S0-BTQ-841

WHAT THIS MODERN JEW BELIEVES

by Rabbi Isaiah Zeldin

This publication made possible by the

Evelyn and Norman Feintech Family Foundation

WHAT
THIS
MODERN
JEW
BELIEVES

by Rabbi Isaiah Zeldin

Isaac Nathan Publishing Co., Inc.

Los Angeles

1996

What This Modern Jew Believes

© Copyright 1996 by Rabbi Isaiah Zeldin

Library of Congress Card Number 96-68430

Library of Congress Cataloging-in-Publication Data
Rabbi Isaiah Zeldin
    What This Modern Jew Believes
        1. Basic Judaism   2. Biography
        3. Jewish Thought   4. Modern Jewish Beliefs
        5. Historical Jewish Beliefs

ISBN 0-914615-01-7

Manufactured in the United States of America

Isaac Nathan Publishing Co., Inc.
22711 Cass Avenue
Woodland Hills, CA 91354
(818) 225-9631 FAX (818) 225-8354

Table of Contents

Dedication

This book is dedicated to my family

for whom I have tried to create

a healthy Jewish environment

by building the many programs

of the

Stephen S. Wise Temple

Preface

Once, when our congregation had recently published a new High Holiday prayer book, a Conservative Rabbinic colleague said to me, "Please send me a copy, so I can criticize it."

This book is meant for lay people. Dates are rounded out, mostly to the nearest century. Biblical characters are quoted in contemporary modes of speech. And sometimes elementary facts are presented mostly for the Jewishly unlearned.

However, the opinions are the results of a lifetime of teaching, first Rabbinic students, then religious school teachers, and mostly adults interested in Jewish issues of a theologic nature.

Some of the chapters herein presented were originally given as lectures to a class of adults studying with me for twenty-one years. That registration in this year-long class has been between three and four hundred people has pleased me immeasurably.

The taped sessions were edited by my publisher who thought to leave them in the conversational tone of the lecture. That was altogether agreeable to me as I edited the transcripts.

I regret the lack of footnotes, but my sabbatical, given to me so I could put together this book, was only of six months duration. My admiration is now increased for those who write books and have the stick-to-it-iveness to finish them.

The opinions offered herein are my own, though I borrowed background material from many authors and scholars. I consider myself a modern Jew and offer like minded modern Jews sufficient reasonings to support what I consider is rapidly becoming the faith of most American Jews.

Isaiah Zeldin

June, 1996

Acknowledgements and Notes

I deeply appreciate the energy and labors of David Epstein, my publisher and Ann Terrick, my secretary who made this work a positive experience.

Author's Notes

I have capitalized the word, "Rabbi," which is contrary to accepted usage. I did so because I believe Rabbis to be preservers of Jewish tradition, especially in the United States. Hence, the title is capitalized to remind the reader of the centrality of the role of Rabbis of whom I am proud to have been part for these past fifty years.

One final note: The chapters on "Beliefs" were originally given as class lectures, hence the many colloquialisms. Perhaps a more formal book is called for—that I have reserved for my next sabbatical.

Chronicles-One

B.S.S.W.T.

Before Stephen S. Wise Temple

LET ME TELL YOU WHO I AM AND HOW I GOT TO BE WHAT I AM. To all who know me I am *Shy* Zeldin. Only telephone solicitors call me Isaiah—my true name. Aside from some biographical information I will include certain incidents from my childhood and family background from which you will be able to understand me and my enthusiasm for all things Jewish.

I was born in Brooklyn on July 11, 1920. I have always considered myself lucky since my birthday is 7-11. Brownsville, where I grew up, was a very Orthodox neighborhood.

My mother was a rather cultured person who read Russian literature, spoke Yiddish, and paid a tutor so she could learn how to write in English. My father was a runaway Tzarist soldier who spoke and wrote Hebrew and was the best Yiddish speaker in Brooklyn.

When my parents met and marriage was in the offing, my father said to my mother, "We will get married only after you learn to speak Hebrew." So my mother took a crash course and learned how to speak Hebrew in six weeks. They both had decided to raise their children in Hebrew, assuming we would learn English on the street. My parents were right about that. Not only did I learn English on the street, but also how to fight back and how to run—fast.

My mother once sent in an anecdote to a Yiddish daily, *Der Tag*, and received $2 for an item called: "Wise Sayings from Children." My youngest brother is almost four years my junior. As an infant, he cried loudly in his crib. My mother had asked me to go to his room and tell him to stop crying. I turned to my mother and said, "How can I do that. I speak Hebrew. The baby doesn't understand a word of Hebrew!"

My father's first job in America was that of a Hebrew teacher. He soon became principal of the Pennsylvania Avenue Talmud Torah, one of the few schools that used Hebrew as the language of instruction.

When Rabbi Stephen S. Wise became President of the Zionist Organization of America, he asked my father to leave his position and become a top executive in that organization. A few years later my father became one of the founders of the United Palestine Appeal, which later became the United Jewish Appeal. He worked as the major fund raiser of the Brooklyn division until his retirement.

My father was a Zionist, a Yiddishist, and a Hebraist. He wrote for both the Yiddish and Hebrew press in America. He was known as a *philatonist*—essentially a propagandist—one who writes articles to present his point of view. From time to time I too became a philatonist.

Although my father was very Orthodox, he had an enlightened view on religion. When Rabbi Mordecai Kaplan published his new Reconstructionist prayer book, some Orthodox Rabbis actually had a book burning ceremony. My father excoriated them in speeches and articles saying: "Who is it that burns books? Anti-Semites and Nazis!

Jews write books and study books." Yet, when the tumult died down, my father wrote another article on why he disliked the new Kaplan prayer book.

When I was 13, in the year 1933, my father took me to a rally-walk protesting the rise of Hitler to power and the nefarious philosophy of Nazism. Leading the rally were Rabbi Stephen S. Wise and the great Unitarian minister John Haynes Holmes. It was at that protest rally that I decided to become a Rabbi so my energies and voice could be influential in the defense of my people.

I graduated from high school when I was sixteen. I wrote to Hebrew Union College, applying to become a Rabbinic student. They replied telling me I was too young and I should first get a college degree.

Both as a high school and college student I was active in the Jewish Culture Council whose aim was to install Hebrew into the curriculum as a recognized foreign language. I remember personally signing up a sufficient number of students so that Brooklyn College could offer Hebrew to a group of twenty-five advanced students. I was one of them.

As I was finishing college, my father discouraged me from applying to the Jewish Theological Seminary (Conservative) and the Jewish Institute of Religion (Reform). He believed graduates of the Hebrew Union College (also Reform) were treated better by their congregants.

✡

In 1945, I was the first to be called in by the president of HUC who asked, "Where would you like to go to fulfill your required second year?" The war was still on and he showed me various places, none of which I had ever heard of: Macon, Georgia; Dothan, Alabama; Columbus, some-place or other; Fort Smith, Arkansas.

The rest of my classmates—only eight of us at the time —were waiting anxiously for me to leave the president's office. My wife Florence was waiting with them. They all asked, "What did he offer you?"

I mentioned the places and nobody knew where any of them were.

Then my wife said, "Didn't he offer someplace else?"

"Yes, he mentioned someplace in California, but I can't remember where."

She said, "Think hard! What did he say?"

"It sounded something like Stockmon, or Stock-ton, or something like that."

We all ran to the library to get an atlas and to look up and see where Stockton was. We read, "Stockton is in the San Jouqain Valley, in California, not far from Fresno. The climate is ideal."

My wife's brother was stationed in Fresno, so she said to me, "Listen, we've got to spend a year and we may as well go to California."

We arrived in Stockton on V.J. Day.

✡

The first week in California, we discovered walnuts on the street. New Yorkers don't see walnuts on the street. So Florence bent down and picked up enough walnuts to fill our pockets.

At our first Friday night service in Stockton, some people came and brought us bags of walnuts. I thanked them very much and asked, "How did you know that we liked walnuts?"

They replied, "It isn't nice for the wife of the Rabbi to pick walnuts up off the street."

Every week after that the people who came from Lodi, a neighboring farm town, brought us bags of walnuts and grapes. Thus was a Rabbi's dignity maintained.

✡

There was also a naval base, an army base, and a prisoner-of-war camp near Stockton. On the very first day in California I received a phone call . . . .

"Rabbi?"

"Yes. "

"My name is Cecil B. Harvey. Glad to meet you."

I said, "Who are you?"

He said, "I'm the Protestant chaplain at the Air base. There are thirteen Protestant chaplains in the area, and there's not one Jewish chaplain. Can I come to see you?"

I said, "Sure."

He came the next day and said, "What I would like to do is dedicate myself to the service of Jewish people in the army. You be the Rabbi, I'll be the Protestant chaplain. We'll have an army car at our disposal. Whatever you want, I'll get for you.

We rapidly became the best of friends. The two of us were the Jewish chaplains for all the Jewish service men within a radius of about 75 miles. Whenever a Jewish serviceman was sick or needed our sevices, we were called and we went.

I thus had access to the Jewish servicemen who were stationed in and around Stockton. After I conducted a service for them at the army base, they would come into town to our Friday night services. As a result, the local Jewish families with eligible daughters came to our services knowing Jewish servicemen would be attending. Our synagogue became the rallying place where Jewish men in the service met Jewish women who lived in Stockton.

The first wedding that I ever officiated at was for a chief petty officer and one of the daughters of a rather affluent local family. They had originally asked for a chaplain to come in from San Francisco. However, the base was run by a Jewish one-star general whose wife was Catholic. The wedding was to be sponsored by the general's wife and catered by the POWs.

She wanted the couple to walk down the aisle under crossed sabers, in fine army tradition. When the San Francisco Jewish chaplin heard about the crossed swords, he suddenly had a grandmother who died in New York and had to leave. I wound up having to officiate.

I said to the general's wife, "I'm terribly sorry, there is a prohibition against bringing swords or instruments of war into our chapel."

The general's wife wasn't pleased, but she had no alternative. I was the only Rabbi around. So we reached a compromise. Since it was army tradition at officer's weddings for the couple to walk under crossed sabers I said, "I'll tell you what we can do. As soon as the couple leaves the chapel, we can have the honor guard outside. Let the couple walk under the crossed sabers outside the chapel." Everybody was happy at the solution.

One incident about this wedding sticks in my mind. They had the German POWs cater the wedding. The POWs

Isaiah
at
Camp Achvah
1941

Florence
at
Camp Achvah
1941

Application
to
Hebrew Union College
1940

Director,
Camp Tall Trees,
Kentucky
Summer,
1945

Isaiah and Florence Zeldin, 1943

— Below —
Rabbi Isaiah Zeldin (r.)
with
Rabbi Jay Kaufman ᴮ˝ᶻ (l.)
on
Graduation Day
and
Ordination from
Hebrew Union College,
1946

— Above —
Rabbi
Zeldin
as
Assistant
Rabbi,
Newark,
N.J.
1948

**Rabbi Zeldin being installed at Temple Emanuel, Los Angeles,
by Dr. Maurice Eisendrath, 1950**

(l. to r.) Michael, Isaiah, Joel, Florence, 1958

(top, l. to r.) Grandparents, Conrad & Sarah Karp, Morris & Esther Zeldin
Isaiah Zeldin, Joel, Michael, Florence Zeldin, 1960, Joel's Bar Mitzvah

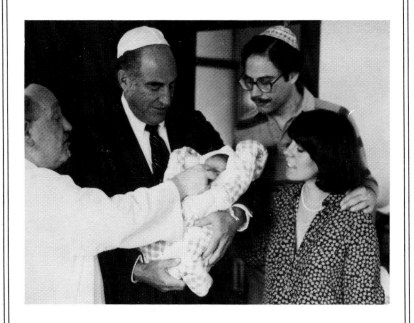

***Brit Mila* of Gabriel Zeldin,
1982
(l. to r.) Mohel, Grandfather Isaiah Zeldin,
Joel & Karen Zeldin**

had prepared chopped liver because they knew Jewish people like it. We finished the wedding, went to the reception, and saw three, five foot high, chopped liver wedding bells.

I heard one POW say to another, in German, "What do you think?"

The other POW, looking at the chopped liver, replied in German with the Yiddish word: *Shreklich* (terrible).

✡

After a year, we went back to HUC in Cincinnati for graduation and for ordination, and then moved to Newark, New Jersey where I was the assistant Rabbi for two years in a very large congregation and got my taste of classic Reform Judaism. The taste was really a distaste because, while the people treated us wonderfully, and I was really happy, the classic Reform services left me cold. Florence and I thought that we should look for a position that was more Jewishly satisfying.

Joshua Loth Leibman, who was the most popular Rabbi of his day, had just published a book, "Peace of Mind," that sold over a million copies. In those days, that meant it was at the top of the best-seller list.

Rabbi Liebman had heard about me and asked if I would become his assistant. I listened to his offer and learned my job would be mostly answering his mail. He must have received 5,000 letters a week because he also had a popular radio program. I was told that when Rabbi Liebman would go on a lecture tour, I would be permitted to do the Saturday morning service, but not the Friday night service. He was a good preacher and would get about a thousand people to attend his Friday night services. I talked it over with my wife and we decided that to be a ghost writer for a prominent person wasn't why I had become a Rabbi. So I turned down his offer.

The proposition had been brought to me by Dr. Abe Franzblau who had been one of my professors at the Hebrew Union College. When I turned down Joshua Leibman's offer, Dr. Franzblau turned to me and said, "How would you like to work for me?"

Dr. Franzblau was a wonderful gentleman, an excellent teacher, a man who, in addition to being a prominent educator, knew psychology and psychiatry well. I asked, "What's the job?"

He replied, "Well, the job is something that I am going to create. I'm the Dean of Hebrew Union College in the New York branch of the school. I want you to be the Assistant Dean. But I can't pay you very much."

So I said, "You mean I will have to get another job to supplement my income?"

He said, "Yes. You will have to get another job."

So I sought and received an appointment as a weekend Rabbi; first in New York City, and then in Flushing, Long Island. I served in the dual positions for five years. During that time, I was left in charge of the entire faculty for HUC's School of Education and the School of Sacred Music. Dr. Franzblau was busy setting up the psychiatry department for Yeshiva University Medical School—now called Albert Einstein Medical School in New York. So there I was, a Rabbi in my twenties running the Hebrew Union College schools in New York.

I fondly remember some of the rather odd things that I did during those years. I figured, that since I was running the school, my job was to supervise the faculty. One of the professors, Theodore Gaster, was an internationally known scholar and author of many books that could fill a whole shelf. Dr. Gaster was a great speaker, an Englishman, a tall impressive individual, but a man whose vocabulary was so extensive that the students couldn't understand some of the things he was saying.

One day, I called him in and politely said, "Dr. Gaster, I have a request to make of you."

He said, "What is it?"

I said, "Some of the students in your classes are complaining that you're talking over their heads."

He stood up, his 6'3" frame towering over me, looked down at me and said sternly, "Rabbi Zeldin, I am speaking where their heads ought to be."

From that moment on I decided that never again would I confront a professor whose reputation was greater than mine.

Because I was the assistant dean, I had the responsibility of assigning who would teach which course. I spent five years at that position. Each semester, I assigned to myself a new course. I wound up teaching in every discipline. I also taught in the cantorial department. Since I had an Orthodox background, I was the liturgist amongst the Reform faculty.

We had such famous cantors as Morris Ganchoff and Israel Efros, and such choir directors as Abe Binder and

Israel Freed. I was usually only one lesson ahead of the students but I worked hard on class preparation and taught myself many things I did not learn as a student at the Hebrew Union College.

Those years made me pound the books and I became a person who, though not an original scholar, knew an awful lot in every department of Jewish scholarship. The constant studying and preparation for teaching have stood me in good stead, because whatever subject in Rabbinics I need to talk about, at one time, I taught the course.

Both of our children were born while I served in the east. Joel in Newark in 1947 and Michael in New York City in 1950.

In 1953, Rabbi Jay Kaufman, who was my closest friend in theology school and was then vice-president of the Union of American Hebrew Congregations and assistant to Dr. Maurice Eisendrath, came to me and said, "The West Coast director of the UAHC has just died. How would you like to be the director of the UAHC out in California."

I replied that I would not like to be the director of the UAHC.

Then Rabbi Kaufman sweetened the offer by adding, "There is a college out there that is run by the Union. It's called the College of Jewish Studies." Immediately my ears perked up.

He continued, "It's not very much of a college, but since you are the only person now in the Reform Rabbinate who knows how to run a college, would you also accept that challenge?"

I replied, "Only if you make that at least fifty percent of my job."

When the details were worked out my family and I moved to California, so I could be the Dean of the College of Jewish Studies run by the Union of American Hebrew Congregations. At the same time I would serve as the West Coast Director of the UAHC. One job would be running a college, while the other one entailed helping the member congregations.

✡

When we moved to L.A. in 1953, I discovered that the college, which met at the Wilshire Boulevard Temple, had but a handful of students. Less than a month later, Rabbi Jay Kaufman wrote me a rather clever letter saying, "Listen *Shy,* I know that the college isn't very much and it's going to be almost impossible to make it succeed. If it fails, we'll understand, and at least you'll be doing the UAHC work.

I decided that the best reply to Jay Kaufman's letter was to put my energy and concentration into making the college succeed.

By the time we finished the first year, we already had a student body of several hundred students and were now teaching teachers how to function better in southland Sunday Schools. They were accredited teachers in the public school system, with little religious or Hebrew knowledge.

We were so successful in that first year that Dr. Nelson Glueck, President of the Hebrew Union College asked whether the College of Jewish Studies could become a branch of the Hebrew Union College.

Maurice Eisendrath said, "Wait a while. We are paying Rabbi Zeldin's full salary. If you, Dr. Glueck, want to run the college as a part of HUC, then you have to pay half of his salary, since half of *Shy's* job is running the college. Dr. Glueck readily agreed.

Later on, in 1958, when there was a struggle regarding who controlled the college, Dr. Eisendrath said that it was one of the worst mistakes he had made—letting Dr. Glueck pay for half my salary because the California college would be dominated by the Hebrew Union College and not by the Union of American Hebrew Congregations.

The first thing I did at the Los Angeles College of Jewish Studies was to institute some of the practices that I knew from the New York school. We assembled an exceptional faculty, including Max Helfman, the outstanding composer of Jewish music and Mr. Sam Kaminker, a gifted Jewish educator employed by the Bureau of Jewish Education.

In a short period of time we had a School of Sacred Music, a Pre-Rabbinic Department and a large School of Education. Our faculty included outstanding non-Jewish teachers who taught in various universities. These were fabulous charismatic personalities. By the second year we had built up a student body of over three hundred students.

Within five years we had a Rabbinic Department. Some of the Rabbis who now serve congregations in the Los Angeles area were the youngsters we recruited to the West Coast branch of the Hebrew Union College.

I left the UAHC and the Hebrew Union College in 1958. Each of my bosses, Dr. Eisendrath and Dr. Glueck, fought to control the college in L.A. I found myself writing two sets of reports on the progress of the college—one I would send on UAHC stationery to New York, and one I would send on HUC stationery to Cincinnati.

A second reason for leaving the Union and the College was the untimely death of Rabbi Bernard Harrison who served Temple Emanuel in Beverly Hills. The congregation asked me to become the Rabbi of the second largest congregation in the Los Angeles area, and I accepted their offer.

That turned out to be a mistake. After having served at Temple Emanuel only two years I knew that the congregation's philosophy did not accord with mine. I always had believed that a Rabbi was the spiritual leader of his congregation. The board of directors thought I was just another employee—no better than the maintenance staff—and they treated me accordingly.

While my relationships with individual members of Temple Emanuel were excellent, the board of the congregation was a constant source of distress. The situation deteriorated and after another three years, a group of families left with me to establish the Stephen S. Wise Temple.

✡

Chronicles-Two
S. S.W.T.
Stephen S. Wise Temple

> Fred Plotkin has edited an excellent history of the first 25 years of the congregation entitled: *"Once Upon a Mountaintop."* I consider that book a companion piece to this work and will not repeat its all-inclusive contents.

STEPHEN S. WISE TEMPLE WAS BORN when thirty-five families met in the home of Ruth and Julian Pregulman, which was on the same block as St. Alban's Church in Westwood, just opposite UCLA. At the very first service, conducted at the end of April 1964, over 185 families attended and joined the new congregation.

Each family that left Temple Emanuel gave up something by leaving such a prestigious congregation. They left a temple that had a building, a large membership and a reputation, in order to come with *Shy* Zeldin who only had himself. The people that first joined Stephen S. Wise Temple were idealistic individuals.

At the end of our first year over 250 families were members of the congregation. We weren't in existence more than half a year when we purchased the land on Mulholland Drive.

The driving person behind the development of our new property—and there were many excellent people—was Norman Feintech. The executive board, which steered our fledgling congregation, included Fred Plotkin, Norman Eichberg, Abe Hershenson, Joe Kleiman, Ben Winters and Harriet Citrin, each capable individuals whose devotion was unmatched. But Norman Feintech, aided by his wife Evelyn, was as devoted to this project as any lay person could possibly be. Norman is a man of great wisdom and real estate experience. It was he who pushed for the purchase and development of our property as quickly as possible. Other congregations have started in Los Angeles, especially on the West Side, but it is very difficult to find a large enough piece of land. When we found that parcel up on Mulholland Drive, Norman and others wholeheartedly threw themselves into the work of grading and erecting our first building.

There was a faction of thirty-five families who said, "But the original families all live in Westwood, Beverly Hills and Brentwood. Why are we going up to the mountains?" Those thirty-five families planned a minority-view meeting in a private home.

When I heard of it I told them, "You can't do this. If you want to have a meeting, have it in the temple office." Abe Hershenson had given us a suite of offices on the top floor of one of his buildings. I said, "If you do it in a private house, then it's clandestine. It sounds as if you're in opposition to the whole project. You have a perfect right to express your opinions. Therefore have it in the temple, invite all the people who will come, and present your point of view at a congregational meeting. That is the way democracy is practiced. When there are two points of view, these should be argued. Once a decision is reached, then only the point that prevails is to be followed."

I remember well the congregational meeting. The faction presented its position and the majority presented its point of view. The meeting lasted well beyond midnight. Somebody stood up and said, "But, Rabbi, it's a small congregation, how can you risk thirty-five families leaving the congregation?"

To which I replied, "I think that would be a tragedy, because that isn't the way Jewish life is conducted. In our tradition, whenever an issue came up and there was a majority and a minority viewpoint; once the decision was made, the minority followed the decision of the majority. My experience as UAHC director showed me that if a congregational dispute occurs, perhaps three families resign. We can't please everybody, but if we wait for unanimity, we will never take an important stand."

The majority position prevailed. Exactly three families resigned, two of which rejoined within the year.

✡

Let me back up a little to relate how we wound up using St. Alban's Church as our first venue for services.

There was a "very wise" committee established by Temple Emanuel to work out the concluding arrangements with me, for I had a contract that still had six months left to run. They stated that they had heard that there was a possibility of my starting a new congregation. They said they would continue to honor my contract if I didn't establish a new congregation within a radius of five miles of Temple Emanuel. I had already, together with Fred Plotkin, traveled the distance between Temple Emanuel and St. Alban's Church, and we had measured it as 4.7 miles.

So I lightheartedly said, "Instead of five miles, let's make it 4.7."

Knowing my sense of humor, they graciously said, "Sure, we'll make it 4.7 miles."

Little did they know that the very first service that we had as Stephen S. Wise Temple would be attended by over three hundred people in St Alban's Church, just 4.7 miles away from Temple Emanuel.

There was supposed to be a letter sent out by Temple Emanuel stating that the reason for my severance was that we differed in philosophy. Unfortunately for them, they kept the pot boiling and spread rumors of my wrong doings. Nothing could have served our cause better. With each issue and rumor that they spread, more of their members found their way to our new congregation.

When Stephen S. Wise Temple was about two weeks old, a number of Temple Emanuel's prominent people asked me to a luncheon. They had heard of our success. The sum and substance of the luncheon was, "Rabbi Zeldin, what would it take to come back and be the Rabbi of Temple Emanuel?"

I replied, "Well, you know that I only make 50% of the decision. I'll have to consult with my wife and will call you tonight to let you know."

I went home, and consulted with my wife, along with Norman Feintech and Syd Dunitz. That night I phoned one of the members of Temple Emanuel's unofficial committee and replied, "You asked what would it take for me to return to Temple Emanuel? . . . not all the tea in China!"

✡

I have learned from the experience that people are not loyal to buildings, but that people are loyal to people. Stephen S. Wise Temple soared past the 900 family mark in about four or five years.

In those days, I used to officiate at weddings and funerals for non-members. I did so at firstl because I needed the income, and secondly, because most of the time when I served a non-member at a wedding or a funeral, by the end of the service, the family became members of Stephen S. Wise Temple.

Many of the early families who joined Stephen S. Wise Temple were people for whom I had done something. The original 185 families were people for whom I had officiated at a function, or were in a class I taught, or had a personal relationship with me from UAHC or HUC days.

As we soared beyond the 900 family members mark, the only people who knew all 900 families were Norman Eichberg, who was the first elected president of the congregation and myself.

Norman and I would stand at the back of the church social hall after services and greet each and every person. One gentleman who came to our service had been a member of the most prominent congregation in Los Angeles for thirty years, yet was not known personally by the Rabbi. When I said *Good Shabbos* to the visitor and his wife, he told me about his anonymity at the other temple.

So I said, "What's your name?"

And he said, "My name is Murray."

"It's nice to meet you Murray."

The next week he showed up again at the back of the *Good Shabbos* greeting line. When he reached me he stuck out his hand.

I greeted him and said, "It's nice to see you again Murray."

"Damn it," he said, "you remembered my name, I'm joining your congregation." That's how we added many new members to our temple family.

✡

Another cause for the success of our new congregation was the excellent schools we founded, right from the outset. The Sunday school, the Hebrew school, and the Confirmation department were the creative products of Metuka Benjamin, who, to this day, is the Educational Director of Stephen S. Wise Temple.

Metuka Benjamin had been a teacher at Temple Emanuel. She was probably the best teacher on their staff. When I left Temple Emanuel, Metuka was pregnant. She had been the teacher of our two sons, both of whom loved her as a teacher and as a person.

We started our congregation in April, 1964 and planned to open our schools in September. I went to Metuka—or perhaps she came to me—but we got together and planned our schools over the summer. Metuka quickly became the director of our schools. Metuka is the longest paid employee of Stephen S. Wise Temple.

✡

For the first year of the congregation I did not take a salary. Even after my contract with Temple Emanuel ran out, I refrained from taking a salary. I did a lot of weddings and funerals and was in great demand as a lecturer. I went to universities and I gave guest talks to other congregations and was thus able to support my family.

At Temple Emanuel the Rabbi was required to turn back fees. At Stephen S. Wise Temple I retained fees earned for my officiating at weddings and funerals. I earned more the first year as a so-called freelance Rabbi than Temple Emanuel had paid me. When I left Temple Emanuel I thought I would be making a financial sacrifice. It did not turn out that way. Stephen S. Wise Temple was like a newborn child that brought its own luck.

The Bible tells that when Samson killed a lion he said, "from the bitter came forth the sweet." I have always believed that my leaving Temple Emanuel was one of the best things that happened in my life. I knew from the start that "from the bitter would come forth the sweet." Now that I had started my own congregation, its failure or success would depend upon me—not on some board deciding my fate.

✡

Rabbi Stephen S. Wise had, in his lifetime, been offered the most important pulpit in the United States—Temple Emanuel in New York City. The chairman of the board of the congregation was a very prominent Jew called Louis Marshall. Rabbi Wise was invited to give a trial sermon at Temple Emanuel. The committee evidently approved of him and was about to offer him the position. Mr. Marshall asked if Rabbi Wise would be good enough, since he was a controversial figure, to submit his sermons to the board before he gave them. Rabbi Wise, who at the time was in Portland, Oregon, had come to New York for the interview and since gone back to Portland. When he learned of the condition attached to the offer he fired back a telegram saying, "I refuse to be ruled by Marshall law." Rabbi Wise then returned to New York and founded the Free Synagogue.

At Temple Emanuel in Beverly Hills there was also a pulpit committee who made life difficult for me by questioning my sermons. When they asked for advance copies of sermons, I told them, "I will give you a copy of my sermons only after they are delivered and I will not discuss them with you beforehand."

✡

At Stephen S. Wise Temple we started the congregation as a "limited" congregation. We were going to limit the membership to 250 families—which we reached before we were a year old. We then raised the limit to 350 and then to 500, then 650, 800, 900. When membership got over a thousand we finally had enough and I said to the congregation, "We're kidding ourselves. We ought to have an open membership." And that's what we did.

✡

When we purchased our present property, we acquired a piece of land that was inaccessible. Casiano Drive was not cut through and the mountain was fifty feet higher than the present property.

Norman Feintech was the expert, *par excellence*, on mountain property. The first thing he did was get an estimate as to how much it would take to "daylight the property." That means, to get enough land that was level. We found out that we would have to move a million cubic yards of dirt.

This was overwhelming for a new congregation and we knew we couldn't do it by ourselves. We had to look around for a partner. I've always had good relationships with the Conservative movement and a good friend of mine was Matthew Berman, who was a key layman in many activities of the Conservative movement.

We met with Matthew and said to him, "We have a piece of property for you to purchase for the University of Judaism." Before long, the University purchased it, and shared equally in the expense of moving the dirt. We moved our mountain—one million cubic yards—down to their property which was mainly a hole much lower than ours. The University of Judaism now rests on, what was originally, our mountain top. We built our first building immediately.

A short time after the properties were graded, the owners donated the approximately six acres of hillside between the properties to both institutions and, after lengthy negotiations, we wound up with Faber Field and they got the corner of Casiano and Mulholland Drive.

Our first building was completed in 1968 when the congregation was about four years old. The first affair at the temple was the upcoming wedding of our son Joel and Karen Dash. The race was on as to whether the building could be completed in time for the wedding, which was to take place on August 18th.

Norman Feintech and the building committee, chaired by Fred Plotkin did everything possible to get the social hall ready by the 18th. On the 16th, we had Hershenson Hall and the attached classrooms almost completed. There were sandbags in place of windows and pulleys holding the beams. There were no bathrooms as yet so we rented portable bathrooms. I called Groman Mortuary and borrowed grass carpeting so we could cover the sand and dirt. People were thus able to walk on the "grass," but we never told them it came from a cemetery.

We didn't have power because we still needed our "certificate of occupancy." It was a Friday afternoon, and the wedding was to take place on Sunday. We needed a building inspector to approve what we had done so we could get power and have the wedding.

A short-wave broadcast went out to all the building inspectors of Los Angeles that said, "if there is an inspector in the neighborhood of Stephen S. Wise Temple, please go and inspect their project for it needs emergency approval. Sure enough, about an hour-and-a-half later, an inspector showed up. It turned out that the inspector was from Pasadena.

When he arrived he said, "Before I look over the property, I have to tell you why I'm here."

So we said, "Fine, tell us."

He continued, "I have a brother in New York who tried to get into college. He had great difficulty getting suitable recommendations. Finally somebody had a connection with Rabbi Stephen S. Wise. Rabbi Wise was always doing things for people and he wrote the recommendation that got my brother into college."

The inspector then added, "When I heard that Stephen S. Wise Temple needed an inspector, I decided to come and pay back my family debt."

The wedding took place but with several complications. We didn't have enough electricity. When we played the organ we had to shut the coffee maker, and when we used the coffee maker, we had to shut the organ.

It took four years from the founding of the congregation to complete our first building. Thereafter, almost every other year we have built an additional building.

One of our members, Marty Friedman, was in the *shmatah* business (garment industry). He gave us our swimming pool. One day he took me aside saying, "Rabbi, I know you have eighteen acres up here, but when you build, build slowly, but build first class."

And that's what we have done. We now have sixteen buildings on our various campuses. We built every building as magnificently as we could, but we did so expeditiously, economically, wisely, and beautifully. The last thing we wanted was ostentatious buildings. Although the buildings were put up one at a time, it is almost impossible to tell which building was put up first and which was last. Everything matches.

✡

In 1970, the congregation negotiated a merger with Westwood Temple and added about 100 families to our membership plus their physical plant that was eventually sold for $500,000.

Westwood Temple had been led by Rabbi Trattner who was an excellent, practical Rabbi, without official ordination. When he died, the congregation could not find a replacement who could keep the congregation solvent. They let it be known that they would like another congregation to merge with them, and we heard that the prime suitor was Temple Emanuel of Beverly Hills.

We approached them and made them the following offer: "We know your current Rabbi wants to become a psychologist. We will pay his salary for five years, and we will continue the same dues structure that you have."

Since we didn't have a brotherhood nor a sisterhood. we said we would let their brotherhood and sisterhood function at Stephen S. Wise Temple and our members would be encouraged to join.

Their groups had a number of wonderful people. One was Tillie Citron, a fabulous woman who helped sell the idea of the merger. Mary Witzman was a positive woman who impressed all our younger women. The Leffs, Lou and Sybil, were very active and natural leaders. And one of their members, Les Surlow, rose to become president of our merged congregation in just a few years.

We were as gracious as we possibly could be. Since we did not wish to dominate or submerge them, we integrated their families rather quickly and to this day many of them are active members of our congregation.

When we looked about for somebody to buy their building we found that the State of California was interested in putting a freeway through Westwood. We then convinced the State of California to buy the property which they did before they realized that the neighbors would object and the freeway would never be built along Santa Monica Boulevard.

The money we realized from the state was the impetus for the fundraising toward the construction of our main sanctuary which is called the Westwood Sanctuary.

As the congregation grew, I quickly realized that I couldn't be the sole Rabbi running what was humorously called a one-man store. We have had various assistant Rabbis, but somehow, we never found the right individual who would stay. Our assistant Rabbis were capable people, but they would not function as team players.

Our son Michael had gotten to know Eli Herscher at Camp Swig. Eli was a graduating Rabbinic student. We interviewed Eli and believed he was just the right Rabbi for us. When Eli joined the clergy at Stephen S. Wise we knew he would remain for many years. One year later, our staff was enriched again when Cantor Nathan Lam was invited to join us.

Rabbi Herscher joined the staff in 1975, and Cantor Lam in 1976. These two have become good friends and co-workers and are responsible for some of the most innovative services that a congregation can offer.

By 1975 our nursery school had grown by leaps and bounds and our day school had begun. It happened coincidentally with the beginning of school busing. I had always wanted a day school and we had a kindergarten for several years before we attempted to run a day school.

There was a city-wide school called Heschel Day School. Heschel when it started up had three sources for its student body. One was Stephen S. Wise Temple, one was Valley Beth Shalom in Encino and the third was Adat Ari El in North Hollywood. We were part of Heschel for about two or three years, not having enough students to start our own grade one. The busing controversy gave us the impetus to recruit a sufficient number of students to guarantee a first grade of our own.

Very quickly, the day school thrived and we went to grade two, three . . . all the way up to the sixth grade. We had had one of the largest Hebrew schools in the city and now we were on the way to developing the largest day school in the city and the largest one in the U.S. by the late 1970s.

We had hit a plateau at about 1300 families and had been at that plateau for about four or five years. When we announced the day school, we set as a condition of enrollment that the student's family had to join the congregation.

From then on we grew and grew. As soon as we had a sizable registration in the sixth grade, we opened a seventh grade, then an eighth. All the other Reform day schools stopped at grade six. When the time came a couple of years ago to develop our high school we went on to grades nine through twelve. The nursery school grew to an enrollment of about 400 youngsters. Add to this 750 students in grades K-6, and over 400 teenagers in grades seven thru twelve—our enrollment in full time students is over 1550.

Today we have a staff of over 200 teachers. With custodians, Cantors, Rabbis, specialists in music and dance and art and athletics, and secretaries, it adds up to over 400 Temple employees.

The philosophy of the Stephen S. Wise Temple has always been that whatever we can do for Jewish education is worth the effort, the sacrifice, and the struggle. Since the goal is worthy, we are willing to pay the price, and the price sometimes is temporary deficits and large mortgages.

✡

Now we are approaching the 21st century.

We have been called the most active congregation in America. Stephen S. Wise Temple has innovated many programs that congregations across the land are attempting to duplicate. Not the least of these are the Holiday Workshop programs, the Parenting Center and the Saturday morning minyan. Metuka Benjamin, Daphne Pressnell, Howard Lessner, Marilyn Brown, Norma Freeman and Patti Golden are the people responsible for the excellence of the educational programs of our congregation.

But for the first time in the city of Los Angeles, the Jewish population is diminishing. For the first time in American Jewish history there is the prospect of a diminution of the American Jewish population. For the first time in American Jewish history, projecting figures to the year 2020, we see a greatly reduced Jewish community.

Intermarriage is at 52%. Only 28% of those who intermarry raise their children Jewish. That means that 72% do not. A congregation must confront these facts by developing programs to reverse the impact of negative demographics. What is happening to family life in America generally and Jewish family life in particular, is threatening.

Most congregations cater to husband, wife and children families. But the family, as it is now constituted, has many different configurations. We need different programs for single parents, for widows and widowers, for blended families, for step-families, for adopted families and for the great number of single people in the Jewish community.

The Reform congregation cannot serve only upper-class Jewish families that can afford temple memberships. We will need to restructure our dues so that working-class Jews can join, so that middle-class Jews can participate, and we will have to make allowances for poor Jews who today cannot afford to belong to congregations.

We are not a country club which restricts its activities to those who are full dues paying members. We are a Jewish congregation looking out for the welfare of the Jewish community of the future.

The Rabbi is the one who projects the structure and the program in its intricate details, but the board makes the final decision. A harmonious congregation essentially supports the board, even though a lot of the things that will be happening in the future may not be agreeable to people who like the idea of exclusivity.

Let no one imagine that my desire is to become larger. We are probably the largest congregation in the United States. We already have the largest budget. Now we need even more imaginative programming to preserve the Jewish community of the future.

Let me cite one other example of what our congregation does for intermarried couples. We are amongst the most welcoming congregation that strives to make the intermarried couple feel at home in our midst. There are no restrictions on membership and children of mixed parentage are accepted without conditions. We have a new definition of who is a Jew: We don't say to the non-Jewish partner that you must convert to Judaism. Be whatever you wish, just see to it that the family and the household is Jewish. Raise your children Jewish. That's where our future is. The future of the Jewish community in the United States depends upon how intermarried couples will raise their children.

✡

When I was installed at Temple Emanuel, 38 years ago, I remarked in my sermon, that sermonizing is easy, but living according to what one says is the hardest. I believe my family has always been a role model family, which is immodestly my greatest achievement. It really isn't mine alone. It is essentially my wife's. A Rabbi is pulled in many different directions. My wife spent her energies keeping our family intact and stable. That our children are what they are is really to her credit. That our children teach their children a sense of values is also to her credit. I talk it. She does it. She does the hard part.

✡

A great source of satisfaction to me is that we are one of the most nourishing, sustaining, networking congregations in the west. Few can match what we do in caring for individuals.

I attended an affair of Israelis who raise funds to bring sick Israeli children, who cannot be treated in Israel, to America. America has the medical facilities to do what cannot be done even in Israel.

A fifteen-year-old Israeli needed a lung transplant that could be done only here in the United States. The fifteen-year-old youngster had to remain in the United States for six months. The doctors here had to watch him for that length of time if he was to be kept alive.

I learned about the situation from the Israeli Consul General who told us the boy had three other siblings. The three other children and the parents would be coming to the United States and would have to be here for the six months.

Without having to ask the board, I was able to say that we'd take those children into our schools—free of charge. When I asked Metuka Benjamin, our Educational Director, she replied, "We are a caring congregation."

✡

My daughter-in-law, Rabbi Leah Kroll, is the staff person who supervises our Community Action Program. We do *mitzvot* programs that boggle the mind. They are, to me, a great source of pride. While I and Rabbi Herscher concentrate on the internal aspects of Judaism, building up programs and serving our membership, Rabbi Kroll is our emissary to the community. What her committee does in its various enterprises is beyond imagination.

✡

The greatest satisfaction that I have from my work is the personal relationships that my wife and I have built with the membership of the congregation and with the staff. Everyone's family is a part of ours, and our family is a part of theirs. No greater pleasure can a Rabbi have in all of his or her labors.

Rabbi Max Nussbaum once defined a home as, "A home is a place where, if you have to go there, they have to take you in." If you look at the interpersonal relationships in our congregation, what I have tried to do is create an extended family and a Jewish home for the membership.

With my own family I sometimes say, "Do it for my sake." The people I serve know that many times, and in many ways, I do things for their sake.

In Hebrew we say, "One in the mouth and one in the heart." What you feel and what your mouth says have to be the same.

To be a person of integrity is to practice what you preach. If I have had a successful ministry, it is because I have attempted to do just that.

✡

Chapter One
The Periodization of Jewish History
An Introduction

I CAN'T TELL YOU IN SIMPLE TERMS WHAT JEWS BELIEVE on any specific subject because Jewish beliefs have not remained static. Jewish beliefs have constantly changed, usually based on conditions or events experienced during our long history.

For example, if I were to answer the question, "Do Jews believe in Heaven and Hell?" I would have to point out that in our Bible there is no mention of heaven or hell, at least in the way we might talk about it today. The first introduction of Jewish beliefs in an after-life and of heaven and hell began during the Talmudic period, and even included the concept of the *resurrection of the dead.*

When we get to the Modern period, I would say that Reform Jews and most Conservative Jews no longer believe in *resurrection of the dead.* But, I would also say that back in the Biblical period, Jews didn't believe in *resurrection of the dead.* In the Talmudic period we did and in the Medieval period we did.

Unless I make this introduction and tell you what I mean about these various periods, whatever I were to say about Jewish beliefs would be incorrect because it would refer only to a particular period in Jewish history. And since we are modern Jews, we, at least, should be sophisticated enough to understand what I call the *periodization of Jewish history.*

Historical Time Line

1800 B.C.E.	Abraham and Sarah	The *Tanakh*—
1300 B.C.E.	Moses	Biblical
600 B.C.E.	End of the First Temple	Period
200 B.C.E.	Nothing added to the Bible after this point	

∾

100 B.C.E.	End of the Second Temple	The *Talmud*
200 C.E.	The *Mishna* is written	The Talmudic
500 C.E.	The *Gemara* is written	Period

∾

1000 C.E.	End of Babylonian Period	*Responsa*
1500 C.E.	Spanish Golden Age ends	*Literature*
1700 C.E.	Hassidism begins	The Question
1800 C.E.	Reform and Conservative Movements begin	& Answer
1900 C.E.	Birth of Zionism	Period
2000 C.E.	Present Jewish Era	

∾

Most dates in this work are rounded off to the nearest
century. I believe the flow and focus of history is far
more important than specific dates.

Time-Line Chart

So now, like an old fashioned school teacher, I am going to review what I have listed on my time-line chart. This is a historic time-line. We Jews have been in existence for roughly four thousand years and, as such, are the oldest continuous people on the face of the earth.

All other people have changed. The Egyptians today are not the Egyptians of ancient times. The Italians today are not the Romans of Roman times. But we are basically the same Jewish people we were four thousand years ago.

Starting at the top of the chart, we see that Jewish history begins with Abraham and Sarah, not with Adam and Eve or even Noah and his family.

Prehistory and Memory

From a Biblical point of view, there were ten generations between Adam and Eve and Noah. From a modern point of view, all the stories in the Bible through Noah are considered legendary and prehistory.

Similarly, all the stories from Noah to Abraham are legendary. Methusela lived 900 years . . . and so on. The first Jew was Abraham, not Noah. Genesis tells us that Noah was a "righteous man in his generation" to which our Rabbis quickly commented, "Noah was righteous *only* in his generation." Had he lived in the time of Abraham, he would not have been considered so righteous.

Arguing with God

When God said to Noah, "I'm going to bring a flood and destroy everything including human beings," Noah accepted it. That is un-Jewish. To argue with God *is* Jewish.

When Abraham is told by God that God is going to destroy Sodom and Gomorrah, Abraham argues, "But God, what if there are fifty righteous people there?"

And God says, "Okay, if there are fifty I won't destroy it."

"How about forty? Thirty? Twenty?" Abraham continues to bargain with God. Then Abraham says, "God, how can you destroy everying if there are ten? Shall the Judge of all the earth not do justice?"

Ethical Monotheism

Abraham means to say that in the Jewish way of thinking, God cannot do anything that is unjust. This is Judaism's prime contribution to civilization.

We often hear that Jews gave the world monotheism, but that's only half the story. We Jews gave the world *ethical monotheism.*

Recorded History

The first time we see the word "Hebrew" in the Bible is in reference to Abraham. (Gen. 14:13). Abraham, therefore, was the first Jew. Abraham lived before the recorded history of the Jewish people.

According to all current branches of Judaism, Moses is the first person who writes at least part of the Torah. Moses' period is thirteen hundred years before the Common Era which means that the stories of Abraham, Isaac, Jacob and Joseph were carried on by word of mouth for five to six hundred years.

The first record of the Jewish people as a "people" begins with Moses. Most scholars believe he wrote down the Ten Commandments, but Moses is not the only author of the Five Books of Moses. In Hebrew, the Bible is called the *"Tanakh"* an acronym of its three basic sections; *Ta,* meaning *Torah; Na* meaning the *Nevi'im,* Prophets; and *Kh* meaning *Ketuvim* or Writings (TA-NA-KH). The time period of the Bible begins around the year 1800 B.C.E. where our memories began, straight through that line on our chart that says "nothing new added to the Bible," 200 B.C.E., before the Common Era. Its total time covers a period of sixteen hundred years. The physical writing period of the Bible covers a period of eleven hundred years.

Verifiable History

The only evidence we have of Moses is the Bible itself. Most Jews believe that Moses lived, but he is not an "historic" character because we have no other verification. At the end of his life, Moses climbed to the top of Mt. Nebo in Jordan where he looked over the Promised Land and there he died. He never put his foot into the Promised Land. Very wisely, the Bible tells us that nobody knows his burial place. If Moses' burial place had been known, we would have made it a shrine and he would have been considered second to God. In Judaism the belief in one God is even more important than enshrining Moses, the greatest Jewish person who ever lived.

By the time we get to King David, we have actual, verifiable history. King David is an "historic" character because there is evidence, other than the Bible, of his existence.

Moses lived in the period of 1300 B.C.E.. King David lived around the year 1000. The First Temple was built by David's son, Solomon, after the year 1,000 B.C.E., and was destroyed around 600 B.C.E.

When we talk about what Jews believed in the days of the First Temple, we are discussing the four hundred year period from 1000 B.C.E. until the year 600 B.C.E. There were additional things written and put into the Bible down to the year 200 B.C.E., an additional four hundred years. 200 B.C.E. was the cut-off date for material selected for what we know today as the Hebrew Bible.

After that time, whenever a Biblical law needed further explanation, the great teachers would say, "When it says *such-and-such* in the Bible, this is what it means today," and that would update the Biblical ruling.

In a future chapter, when we discuss what Jews believe about, for example, birth control, we will discover that in the time of the Talmud (200 B.C.E. to 500 C.E.) the Rabbis already knew about birth control. They talk about women inserting some kind of a sponge to prevent child birth. We can then compare Jewish beliefs then and now.

The Second Temple

The Second Temple was built in approximately the year 400 B.C.E.. It was destroyed in the year 70 C.E. I put 100 C.E. on the chart to give it round numbers. When we talk about the Second Temple, we refer to that entire five hundred year period. (400 B.C.E. to 100 C.E.)

Those of us who go to Israel and see the Western Wall, which, before the 1967 War was called the "Wailing Wall," are seeing the wall of the Second Temple, just as it was built by one of the Hebrew kings who lived in the period of the Second Temple.

The Talmudic Period

As modern Jews, we have to contrast the Orthodox and the Reform beliefs because there is often a great difference between them. We must understand that any time we refer to the Talmud, it is really the authentic Jewish viewpoint of what the Bible means. We cannot fully understand a specific Biblical law unless we understand the Talmud's explanation of it.

The Talmud, which started as soon as the Bible was ended, continued all the way to the year 500 C.E., covering a period of seven hundred years.

In another chapter we will discuss what Jews believed in the Biblical period about God, and what Jews believed in the Talmudic period about God. And, while a great many things overlap, we will see additions to, and occasionally a substraction from those beliefs.

The Talmud

The Talmud has two sections. One is the *Mishna,* created in Palestine and written in Hebrew. The other is the *Gemara,* written in two places. Some of the *Gemara* was written in Palestine, and, together with the *Mishna,* is called the *Jerusalem Talmud.* The other *Gemara* was written in Babylonia (Iraq) and, along with the *Mishna,* is called the *Babylonian Talmud.* But since the intellectual Jewish community died out in Jerusalem about the year 400 C.E., while Talmudic writing continued in Babylonia until 500 C.E., the *Babylonian Talmud* is considered more authoritative.

Changing Times

When we discuss what Jews believed in the Biblical period, it would be what they believed up until the year 200 B.C.E. Then when we discuss Talmudic times I will show that Jews believed many concepts from the Bible while they changed some others, and they expanded still other concepts.

When Jerusalem was about to be destroyed in the year 70 C.E., Rabbi Yochanan ben Zakkai, escaped and went to the enemy Roman General Titus Flavius Vespasian. He said that he and his disciples would stop fighting if they would be granted the right to establish a school in *Yavneh,* a little town not far from where Tel Aviv is today.

Vespasian was out to destroy the Jewish state. He would have one less group fighting him, so he granted ben Zakkai's request. Little did he know that the *Yavneh* school would outlive the entire Roman Empire.

Judaism's survival depends upon learning and teaching. At the time of Rabbi Yochanan ben Zakkai, we already had organized schools teaching Jewish law as well as the beliefs of Judaism.

Jerusalem was destroyed in 70 C.E. After a second revolution in 135 C.E., most of the Jewish population in Palestine was exiled from their land. Babylonia (Iraq) then became the main center of Jewish learning up until the year 1000 C.E.. The Talmud was finished in the year 500 C.E.

The Period of Responsa

For the next five hundred years, after the completion of the Talmud, when a Rabbi in North Africa was asked a difficult question by one of his followers that he could not answer, he would write to his old teacher, the head of a *yeshiva* in Babylonia. He would ask for his teacher's answer to the question. The Babylonian *yeshivot* were schools for graduate students. The best of these students were ordained Rabbis in their own right.

Starting around 700 C.E., while the Babylonian centers were still important, Jewish colonies began to grow in Spain and Europe. Some of the teachers from Babylonia moved there. By the time we get to the year 1000 C.E., when Babylonia diminished as the major Jewish center, we had fine schools established in Spain. The Spanish Rabbis became the ones to whom other Rabbis wrote when they had difficult questions.

However, the Spanish Rabbis were different from the Babylonian Rabbis and different than the European Rabbis of the year 1000 C.E. who lived in France, Germany and central Europe. (We had not yet gotten to Russia.) The difference was that the Spanish Rabbis were surrounded by an enlightened culture and were educated in many fields in addition to Judaism.

Spain was dominated by the Arabs. But in those days, and I wish I could say it today, the Arabs were enlightened far beyond the Christians. One of the tragedies of today is that the Arabs in the year 1000 C.E. were much more enlightened than many Arabs in the year 2000 C.E., where as Christianity was narrow and limited in the year 1000. Today, close to the year 2000 C.E., Christianity has liberalized itself and is marching essentially in the right direction while much of Islam has retreated from enlightenment.

When Spanish Jews took over the leadership of *yeshivot* in Spain, the Jewish scholars, influenceded by enlightened Arabian culture, became philosophers, poets, and men of science. They were the transition belt between Arabic and Christian civilizations. These great Rabbis enhanced our understanding of Judaism by introducing a new element into Judaism. They introduced the element of Jewish philosophy.

Jewish Philosophy

Jewish philosophy only begins one thousand years ago, not in Biblical times nor in Talmudic times.

The Bible assumes that the reader who opens its pages accepts the idea that there is a God. There are no proofs in all of Biblical literature that there is a God. It assumes there already *is* a God and goes on from there.

The same is true of the Talmud. We see the beginning of arguments for believing in God because later philosophers sometimes built their beliefs about God on Talmudic reasoning.

The use of the rational mind to prove that there is a God began with the Jewish philosophers in Spain and the late Rabbis in Babylonia. It is interesting that at this particular point we also begin to encounter the first Jewish skeptics.

When Maimonides produced his magnum opus, *Guide to the Perplexed*, he was writing to those who doubted the existence of God. The philosophers who added a tremendous dimension to Jewish beliefs attempted to answer the questions of skeptics.

Judaism borrowed philosophical ideas from Christianity and Islam and the greatest of the Jewish philosophers went all the way back to the ancient Greeks, especially Plato and Aristotle.

Judaism has always been an assimilatory faith. We are not immune to outside influences and that is not all bad. We do not say that whatever goes on in the dominant or host culture is of no value to us. Judaism often has taken the best of the general culture and melded it with the best of Jewish culture.

Psychology

Psychology is a comparatively new science and since it has something to contribute to our understanding of human nature, we now have a tremendous number of books that attempt to demonstrate that Judaism already said what psychology books now reveal. Sometimes we even stretch the interpretations a little.

The harmonizing of Jewish thought with the best of contemporary thought began one thousand years ago with the philosophers. When I say that the philosophers added something to our understanding of God, I mean understanding that did not come from our Bible. It also did not come from our Talmud. It came from our Spanish Golden Age.

Jews were exiled from Spain about the year 1500 C.E. (1492). When we were exiled from Spain the center of Jewish learning and culture was lost. What remained was transferred to other places.

Jews in Christian Europe

In Central Europe, as late as 1700, the Jews were still in the Middle Ages, whereas the Jews in Spain were enlightened as far back as the year 1200. Central European Jews were isolated from the Christian communities. For the most part, we lived in rural communities or in cities and towns in *ghettos.*

When we looked around, we saw our Christian neighbors and we saw how unlearned they were. In the year 1700 only about five percent of the Christian public was literate. One of the ways that our people became prominent in the business world was that we were the ones whom Christians sought out to write letters or to read letters and documents. We saw that there was little to learn from Christian culture. It was superstitious and medieval.

Jews of the Middle Ages in Central Europe faced bigotry of all kinds. One thing that allowed our people to survive was, fortunately, that when one little duchy or kingdom would expel its Jews, the one next door would take us in. And then when the new place expelled us, the one from which we came would take us back. The mere fact that Europe was divided into small feudal states made for the survival of our people.

From the Middle Ages up until 1789, most Jews in Europe were living in a narrow strip of land called the Pale of Settlement, with Russia on one side and Germany, Poland, Austria, and Hungary on the other. It was in that narrow strip, where we were constantly fighting against anti-Semites, that we developed various kinds of religious movements that further enhanced our understanding of God.

Mysticism

Mysticism is a product of the Middle Ages. There is a theory which teaches that when external conditions were difficult and there seemed to be no way out of the troubles of the times, Jews turned inward to *mysticism* and found consolation in trying to develop special relationships to God. I am not a mystic but I realize that some Jews, even today, explore that approach. To me it is an escape from facing the realities of everyday living with its inherent problems.

Hassidism

One of these late Medieval developments was the *Hassidic* movement, an Orthodox movement that was dissatisfied with the way Judaism was being practiced by the Rabbis and intellectual Jews. The *Hassidim* saw these Rabbis debating the minutest points of Jewish law, and concentrating on seemingly insignificant details. To the Bal Shem Tov, the originator of *Hassidism* it appeared that they had forgotten what belief in God was all about.

He developed a different approach to Judaism, celebrated with joyousness, with singing and with dancing. *Hassidism,* made a common folk contribution to the idea of God and the relationship of each individual to God.

According to the Orthodox, the way we were to observe God's laws was to follow whatever the Rabbis interpreted. To the *Hassidic* Jew, it depended more upon how we felt, our passion and our enthusiasm. The difference between *Rabbinism* and *Hassidism* was that one was observing while the other was celebrating. Though it never captured the majority of the Jewish people, *Hassidism* made a tremendous contribution to modern Judaism.

The Modern Period Begins

Now we reach the year 1800 C.E. Many Jews living west of the Pale of Settlement—in Germany, France, and Austria and later England and America, came to the conclusion that Orthodox Judaism was too rigorous in its observance of the Jewish Law. They decided that Jews had to enter what was then turning out to be the Modern period. In the year 1800 C.E., (1815 to be exact) we had the beginning of the Reform Movement. The Reform

Movement, to which our congregation belongs, is comparatively new. It is only two hundred years old!

The Conservative Movement is even younger; less than one hundred and fifty years old. The early members of the Conservative movement also wanted to ease the rigors of Jewish Law. However, when they observed Reform Judaism, they believed that Reform had gone too far. Conservative Judaism is essentially a reaction against the extremes of Reform; mostly centered on the breaking away from Orthodox Jewish Law.

In the process of breaking with Jewish Law, Reform Judaism began to develop new ideas about God. According to the Orthodox tradition, when God gave the Torah to Moses on Mount Sinai, all of the further interpretations that we find in the Bible, Talmud, and even Responsa had already been explained to Moses. Moses had taught it to Joshua, who taught it to the prophets, who taught it to the men of the Great Assembly, who eventually became the great Rabbis. According to Orthodox belief, Jews have to observe all the minutiae of Jewish law because this is what God commanded Moses.

Reform Judaism believes that the Torah, and all the books that come afterwards are a *continuous revelation.* It is not a one-time revelation where God said to Moses, "This is Judaism and you observe it for all time."

The minute we say Torah is a *continuous revelation,* it means that leaders and thinkers and scholars in each generation can further develop and further interpret Judaism. However, when we state this, we already question the traditional belief about God and then we have to explain what we no longer believe anymore.

When the Bible says that God performed a miracle, and we now look at it from a modern point of view, we might say that this story was written many years, sometimes hundreds of years, after the event. Then, looking back upon the event, it may have appeared to be a miracle but it was really written by a person with great imagination. Miracles, as supernatural events, tend to go against contemporary thinking.

If God created the universe and the universe has certain laws, for God to want to suspend or change those laws would mean that when God made those laws in the first place, they were not very good laws to begin with. If they weren't very good laws to begin with, then perhaps God wasn't so wise. And if God wasn't so wise, why are we calling Him God? Therefore we find that when we get to the Reform and Conservative movements, we already question supernatural events in our Bible as well as what kind of God is our Creator.

Zionism

Zionism is another of the movements in Judaism that developed in the late 19th century, focusing on the re-birth of a Jewish homeland, preferably in Palestine. Zionism also comes into play with regard to belief in God.

Many visitors to Israel go to a neighborhood called *Meya Shiarim*, the home of ultra-Orthodox Jews. Many of the ultra-Orthodox are anti-Zionist. Ultra-Orthodoxy believes that God will set the world right when He is ready. God will send a messiah *(meshiach)* and the *meshiach* will see to it that evil is eradicated, that peace is established, and that the world will live in brotherhood.

But if I, as an individual, want to establish a State of Israel and do what the *meshiach* should be doing, then I am usurping God's tasks. Therefore, many of these ultra-Orthodox are anti-Zionist. They are saying "who needs a man-made state, if the man-made state is contrary to what we consider to be the classic Jewish teaching about God."

Conclusion

Here we are now, almost at the year 2000. If I describe what Jews believe, I have to take us through the Biblical period, the Talmudic period, the Spanish Golden Age, the period of the Mysticism and Hassidism, the period of early Reform and Conservatism to the present.

✡

Chapter Two
Who Wrote the Hebrew Bible?

I BELIEVE THAT THE BIBLE IS A HUMAN DOCUMENT. It is not a God-written document, although I believe it is a God-inspired document. If the Bible was written by human hands, than obviously, it is subject to mistakes, various versions, and many other things.

There are two different Biblical stories about Abraham and Sarah that tell of the same event but with differences in nuances. See if you can come to the same conclusions that modern scholars have after studying these two versions.

Story #1

The shorter story starts with chapter 12, verse 10 of the *Book of Genesis. (Genesis 12:10)*

> There was a famine in the land and *Abram* went down to Egypt to sojourn there. For the famine was severe in the land. As he was about to enter Egypt, he said to his wife, *Sarai,* "I know what a beautiful woman you are. If the Egyptians see you and think you are my wife, they will kill me and let you live. Please say that you are my sister. Then it may go well with me because of you and that I remain alive thanks to you."

When Abram entered Egypt, the Egyptians saw how very beautiful the woman was. Pharoah's courtiers saw her and praised her to Pharoah and the woman was taken into Pharoah's palace. And because of her it went well with *Abram.* He acquired sheep, oxen, asses, male and female slaves, she-asses and camels.

But the Lord afflicted Pharoah and his household with the mighty plagues on account of *Sarai,* the wife of *Abram.*

Pharoah sent for *Abram* and said, "What is this that you have done to me? Why didn't you tell me that she was your wife? Why did you say that she is my sister? So I took her as my wife. Now, here is your wife, take her and be gone."

There was no equivocating. Pharoah logically believed *Sarai* was one of his concubines. When he discovered the truth, Pharoah put men in charge of *Abram* and sent him off with his wife and all that he possessed. Some might say that *Abram* had made a good deal.

Story #2

The longer story starts in Genesis, chapter 20. *Abraham* had journeyed to the region of the Negev, which is south of Canaan, whereas Egypt is to the West.

There he settled between Kodash and Shur. While he was sojourning in Gerar, *Abraham* said of *Sarah,* his wife, "She is my sister." So *Abimelach,* King of Gerar, had *Sarah* brought to him.

But God came to *Abimelach* in a dream by night and said to him, "You ought to die because of the woman you have taken.,because she is a married woman."

The sentence of the story tells us that when *Sarah* entered his house, all the women became barren—for the

Lord had closed fast every womb of the household of *Abimelach* because of *Sarah*, the wife of *Abraham*.

And *Abimelach* had not approached her. He said, "O Lord, will you slay people even though innocent? He himself said to me, 'she is my sister.' And she also said, 'he is my brother.' When I did this my heart was blameless and my hands were clean.

And God said to him in the dream, "I knew that you did this with a blameless heart and so I kept you from sinning against me. That was why I did not let your touch her. Therefore, restore the man's wife since he is a prophet. He will intercede for you to save your life which means I won't plague you. If you fail to restore her, know that you shall die, you and all that are yours.

Early next morning *Abimelach* called all his servants and told them all that had happened and the men were greatly frightened. Then *Abimelach* summoned *Abraham* and said to him, "What have you done to us? What wrong have I done you that you should bring so great a guilt upon me and my kingdom? You have done to me things that ought not to be done. What then," *Abemelach* demanded of *Abraham*, "was your purpose in doing this thing?

"I thought," said *Abraham*, "surely there is no fear of God in this place and you will kill me because of my beautiful wife and besides, she is in truth my sister, my father's daughter, though not my mother's. She is my half-sister. And she became my wife. So when God made me wander from my father's house I said to her, let this be the kindness that you shall do me. Whatever place we come to, say there of me, he is my brother."

So *Abimelach* took sheep, oxen, male and female, slaves and gave them to *Abraham* and restored his wife *Sarah* to him.

And *Abimelach* said, "Here my land is before you. Settle wherever you please."

And to *Sarah* he said, "I herewith give your brother a thousand pieces of silver. This will serve you as vindication before all who are with you and you are cleaned before everyone."

Abraham then prayed to God and God healed *Abimelach* and his wife and his slave girls so that they bore children."

Now we see, of course, that this is almost the same story as the first shorter one. To the Orthodox Jew this is easily explained: It simply happened twice to Abraham and Sarah. The story is actually repeated a third time, this time about *Isaac* and *Rebecca* (Genesis 26:6).

We have to ask, of the first two versions, which is the older one? The answer has to be the first and shorter version because:

1. He is called *Abram* in the Bible before his name is changed to *Abraham;*

2. In the first story there is no excuse given for what *Abram* says. The first version is the unadulterated version while the second version is the "cleaned up" one;

3. Angels [through dreams] come into the story in the second version. Scholars understand that every time we get two versions of the same story, if one has an angel, then it is the later version.

4. The length of the story also tells us that the first story is the original. When a story is repeated over and over it tends to get longer and longer.

So we can safely say that the *Abram* story was written first and the second, longer version at a later time.

Time Sequence in the Bible

In the *Book of Exodus, Chapter 24,* God says to Moses, "Go up to the mountain and stay on the mountain forty days and forty nights and I will give you . . . [the Ten Commandments]."

But the Ten Commandments had already been given in *Exodus, Chapter 20.* God, therefore, tells *Moses* to go up to get the Ten Commandments four chapters **after** he had already received them.

Don't think that it is only modern scholars who conclude that there is something out of sequence here. Our great commentators *Rashi* and *Maimonides* wrote that in order for the Bible to have been written by God, there could be no such thing as time sequence. There could be no such thing as something that comes earlier and something that comes later in the Torah. This tells me that they really understood that the Torah was a human document and that it was carried on by word of mouth and taught from generation to generation until it was finally edited and written down.

Abraham lived about the year 1800 B.C.E. *Moses* lived about the year 1300 B.C.E. In other words, *Moses* lived five hundred years after *Abraham.* Since the story of *Abraham* was part of the Torah given to *Moses* at Sinai, we have to conclude that for five hundred years, the stories about *Abraham* were told by word of mouth.

Who Wrote Down the Torah

When we carefully read the *Five Books of Moses,* where God teaches the laws to *Moses,* He gives him the Ten Commandments, but He says to *Moses,* "*Moses,* I want you to remember all the other teachings and when you go down from the mountain, that is when I want you to write the Torah." In other words, in the Torah itself, there are various opinions as to who wrote the Torah.

1. One is that God wrote it himself;

2. The second is God dictated it to Moses and Moses wrote it down while on the mountain;

3. God told it to *Moses* and *Moses* wrote it after he came down from the mountain.

It is clear to anybody who really has a sense of literature and a sense of history that the stories of *Abraham, Isaac, Jacob,* and *Joseph,* happened long before *Moses* and had to have been known by him in story form.

Different Schools with Different Stories

Looking back at the *"She Is My Sister"* story, we have to look at the three different versions. It is obvious that these three tales were carried on by different schools who told it orally to their disciples who later repeated it orally to their disciples.

The Biblical editors didn't know which was the correct version, so they included all three. From this we can conclude that the Torah and the Bible are composites, the work of many people over a very long period.

In the oral tradition, from *Abraham* until *Moses,* five hundred years pass before anything is written down. It is another fourteen hundred years before our early Rabbis, in 100 C.E. decided not to include any stories or material written after 200 B.C.E. in their "putting together" of the Bible. This implies that most of the Bible was written and told in story form from 1800 B.C.E. to the year 200 B.C.E. or over a total period of 1600 years.

We have to understand that this does not diminish from the greatness of the Torah and Bible. It just makes it a product of our people. And this product of our people is the product of many individuals.

Our people were inspired people. They were great people. They wrote of values many of which are as valid for us today as when they were first written down.

Times Do Change

But we also must understand that sometimes they wrote of things that were only the product of their times. These things point to what the practices were in those days and, in many cases, we have long since outgrown them.

So, when someone is Orthodox in Judaism, or fundamentalist in Christianity, and says that the Bible is the Word of God, we have to question it. We have to point out that in Biblical days, the God-inspired people who wrote and then assembled our Holy Scriptures also believed many things we don't believe in today.

In Biblical days our forefathers believed in animal sacrifices. We do not believe in that today. Our forefathers believed that homosexuality was a moral evil. We have serious problems with that today. Our forefathers believed that witches were sorcerers and should be killed. We don't believe that today.

In Biblical days, even *Moses* could say that if we have a rebellious and gluttonous son, we should kill him. (I know some modern parents who feel that way.) But our Rabbis of the Talmudic Period looked at this verse and said, point blank, that nobody in Jewish history had ever killed his son or daughter for being rebellious and gluttonous. They had no way of knowing that. They simply understood that this idea didn't work any longer. In other words, even our sages understood, that some things the Torah and the Bible taught were products of their time.

To the modern Jew and to the serious scholar it is clear that the Laws of Moses originated with *Moses* and certainly *Moses* must have promulgated not only the Ten Commandments but also many laws in the chapters afterwards. How those laws were carried out were later decided by the Judges that followed after *Moses.*

We know that Judaism kept adding new interpretations to the Laws of Moses. First our prophets added and then our scribes added and then our Rabbis added something. Even Orthodox Rabbis are aware that Jewish law is at least partially man-made because there are laws and practices in the Talmud where our sages actually voted in order to decide what the Law was.

When, in the year 100 B.C.E., the *School of Hillel* taught one set of principles, and the *School of Shammai* taught another, the final decision followed the majority of the voting Rabbis as to whose interpretation was to be the Law.

When we are told that the Law came from *Moses* in Sinai, we say it lovingly, with tongue in cheek.

The Sequence of the Bible as a Scholarly Tool

I want to go a step further and demonstrate how the rest of the Bible was put together, sometimes out of sequence and sometimes even out of historic fact.

The Book of Joshua

When *Moses* died his successor was *Joshua*, his loyal military leader. The first book in the Bible after the *Five Books of Moses* is the *Book of Joshua*.

In this book, *Joshua* surrounds the city of Jericho and captures it when "the walls came tumbling down." The *Book of Joshua*, the first book after the Torah, tells us that Joshua then conquered the rest of the land and divided it amongst the twelve tribes of Israel.

The Book of Judges

The next book in the Bible after *Joshua* is the *Book of Judges*. Strangely enough, the *Book of Judges* says, ". . . but these are the lands that Joshua did not conquer."

God then appoints Judges to lead the people. Acually, these Judges were military leaders. The military leader became Judge because he (or she) controlled the army. When somebody had a quarrel and came to him (or her) for a decision, he/she would proclaim, "This is the Law." Since he/she had the army to enforce the decision, it usually became the Law.

As we read the literature and understand that the *Book of Judges* is an ancient piece, it begins to sound like other time-honored literary works, such as *Beowulf*. It has some wild stories.

One of the Judges promises God, "If You, God, make me victorious in this battle then the first thing that comes out of my house I will sacrifice to you." He wins, and who walks out of his house? His own daughter.

One of the Judges had a fancy for women. He had long hair, and was a hippie in his day. Samson was his name. And what we learn from this tale is that every Samson has his Delilah.

Deborah was a Judge. Her tale describes a wild, untamed period. When we read the *Book of Judges* we see that people could not travel on the main roads because they would be overtaken by robbers. So people went by "crooked paths" if they had to go from one place to another.

But when we first read the *Book of Joshua*, which tells about the same time period, we are told that Joshua had conquered the land. The Israelites were supposed to be in control.

Scholars conclude, therefore, that the *Book of Judges* was written *before* the *Book of Joshua*. It reflects more accurately the times *before* Joshua conquered the land. The *Book of Judges* tells its stories in natural form, while the *Book of Joshua* relies on miracles added with the passage of time, embellishment, legend and imagination.

But then we have to question whether the Torah, the *Five Books of Moses*, was also put together long after Moses and Sinai.

Rediscovering the Torah

It is strange that in all of the Bible after the Five Books of Moses, we have no reference whatsoever to there being a

Torah until we get to the the middle of the 600's B.C.E..
It is then that King Josiah discovers a copy of the Torah
and begins to have it taught to the people. This indicates
that the people didn't know what the Torah was until
about the year 650 B.C.E..

We know that there was a scribe by the name of Ezra
200 years later, (450 B.C.E.) who, for the first time, de-
creed that every Monday and Thursday the Torah, which
nobody knew in the year 450 B.C.E., should be read in
the market places. That was when people came to town
for the market days. We have to conclude that for the first
time, in 450 B.C.E., our people began to hear the Torah
and to study it.

Comparing Two More Biblical Books

Now let me discuss how modern scholars look at two
other books in our Bible, the *Books of Samuel* and the
Books of Kings, that cover approximately the same period of time, Each consists of two books, *Samuel I* and
Samuel II; Kings I and *Kings II*. Originally each was one
book, but they were so long that they were difficult to
contain in one scroll. Hence, they were each divided into
two books.

Samuel I and II

The *Book of Samuel* tells about King Saul and King David
and ends with King Solomon. Here we are dealing with
actual history. We have archeological proof as well as
other evidence. When we read about *Abraham, Isaac,
Jacob* and *Moses* there is no archeological evidence that
they existed, and our only evidence is in Hebrew scripture.

The kings of the *Books of Samuel* lived between the year 1000 and 900 B.C.E.. It is now presumed that the person who wrote it was a contemporary of King David. The Bible gives us two different versions as to how Saul was annointed as the first Jewish king. The author must have heard two different stories and didn't know which was correct. Since the author was probably very young at the time that Saul accepted the throne, he included both versions in the book.

When we get to King David, the writer gives us the most intimate details imaginable. He even tells us what is going on in David's bedroom as well as in his childrens' love lives. We have to conclude that he was an accurate as well as a sensitive historian. He was a man who must have dearly loved David and yet he tells about David's faults. He doesn't try to whitewash David. It is about as accurate a history as we could possibly get.

Kings I and II

It is much different when we study the *Book of Kings*. The *Book of Kings* starts with King Solomon, who is David's son. Solomon lived around the year 950 B.C.E.. The *Book of Kings* goes all the way to the destruction of the First Temple in the year 600 B.C.E.. That means that the author or authors who put together the books had three hundred years of history to cover. The *Book of Kings* had to be written or edited, not in Solomon's time, but when the last king served almost three hundred years later.

In the *Book of Kings*, we not only have angels but even the Prophet Elijah who goes to heaven riding a chariot.

So now you understand why the *Book of Kings* is less historically accurate than the *Book of Samuel*. Remember the general rule that the longer the period of time that a story has to be told, the more of a *bubba maysa* it tends to become. A *bubba mayse*—a grandmother's tale—is a good place for angels.

The modern scholarly viewpoint is that the contents of the *Book of Kings* were told orally and eventually written down by the school of the prophets. The prophets had a very specific agenda. Simply stated:

1. If a king followed the God of Israel then he is a good king;

2. However, if a king allowed or introduced idol worship into the kingdom, then he is a bad king.

This is the sole criteria as to whether a king is good or bad in the *Book of Kings*.

We now know that there were certain kings who expanded the horizon of the country, who made peace with their enemies. Although they were good kings politically and economically, the *Book of Kings* says that they were bad kings because pagan practices were introduced. Judaism would have died out if this paganism was tolerated, hence, our prophets inveighed against them.

Chronicles

There is another Biblical book called *Chronicles which* covers the same period as the *Book of Kings*. *Chronicles I & II* are written without interesting detail and are mostly dry and dull books. Scholars believe that they tell the history of the Hebrew people as written by court scribes.

These were people who were engaged by kings to write the history of the period. So they wrote it, dully, uninspiringly, and with unimportant details. The personal intimate details that make the *Books of Samuel* come alive and teach moral lessons are absent from *Chronicles.*

When we study the Prophets we find there are certain books that are not the works of one author. The best example is the Book of Isaiah. Isaiah lived approximately in the year 750 B.C.E.. He observed two evils:

1. The people were forsaking the God of Israel;

2. The people were not observing the morality of the teachings of Moses. They were being unjust and oppressing the poor, the widowed, and the fatherless.

This irked Isaiah, so he spoke against the people who committed these offenses. He said that if they continued this way they would be destroyed.

However, when we move to Chapter 40 Isaiah is no longer telling the people to be good or God will destroy them. He now says:

Comfort ye my people. You have paid for your sins already. You have paid more than you deserve for your offenses, and God will restore you to the land.

We know that these well-known words were written after our First Temple was destroyed around 600 B.C.E.. This means that the author who wrote Chapters 40 to at least Chapter 55 of the *Book of Isaiah* lived one hundred-fifty years after the author of the first part. His theme is different. His language is different. His teaching is different. The *Book of Isaiah* really contains the teachings of at least two "Isaiahs."

The Book of Jonah

Within the *Books of the Prophets* there is a little book called the *Book of Jonah*, a charming tale of four chapters.

Prophets believed that they were called by God. Therefore we say their books were "authored by people and inspired by God."

God speaks to Jonah and says, "Jonah, I want you to go to Nineveh." Nineveh was a Babylonian city. Jews had no reason to go there. It was enemy territory.

God continues, "Go to Nineveh, which is a wicked city, and tell them to repent. And if they repent I am going to forgive them."

And Jonah probably said to himself, "They are my enemies. I don't want God to forgive these people. I would rather that He destroy the city."

So Jonah goes out to the sea in the opposite direction. Everyone knows the story. It is the biggest fish story in the Bible. And it is just that. Jonah finds himself in the belly of a whale, After three days the whale spews him out, and the poor guy finally goes to Nineveh. When he gets to Nineveh the people repent, and are forgiven.

A few years ago I participated in a *Book of Jonah* seminar at the University of Judaism with an Orthodox and a Conservative Rabbi. Because my name is Zeldin, they called on me last—which was good.

In great scholarly fashion, each of the other two Rabbis explained that the reason that the book was placed in our Bible and is read on the afternoon of Yom Kippur is to teach the great Jewish concept that repentance is available, not only to Jewish people, but to non-Jews as well. Both the Orthodox and the Conservative Rabbis gave a moral explanation.

Then they called on me. Since this was the University of Judaism, a Conservative institution, I said to them, "Now listen. I'm a Reform Rabbi. So whatever I say, I say for myself. I don't want to convince anybody.

"I honestly believe that this is a story that some very imaginative individual thought up in his mind and wrote down. And it does have that teaching that each Rabbi here has expressed—that *repentance* is available to anybody.

"But it has an even greater teaching. If it were only about the teaching of *repentance,* I don't believe it would have been included in the Prophetic section of our Bible. There are three sections of our Bible; the *Torah,* the *Prophets* and the *Writings.* If the lesson was only on *repentance,* the *Book of Jonah* would have been part of the third section, the *Writings.* But, because it is in the second section, the *Prophets,* indicates that the one who wrote the book must have meant to teach us a lesson about the prophets.

What is the lesson? God says to Jonah, "Go, this is your mission in life." Jonah doesn't want this mission. He is acting like Moses in his day. Remember God said to *Moses,* "Go to Egypt."

Moses said, "Don't send me. Send somebody else."

"The prophet would rather live his own private life. He would like to enjoy it like everybody else. But what makes him a prophet is that **he can't escape.** That is what the word prophet means—his message wells forth from within himself. Even when Jonah found himself in the belly of the whale, he had to go and do what God asked him to do. That, I believe, is the purpose of the *Book of Jonah*. That is why *Jonah* was put in the Prophets' section.

The Book of Job

Let me give you another example—the *Book of Job*. Here is one of the most thoughtful, philosophic books in Biblical literature. There is the story in chapters 1, 2 and 42.

In the first chapter, God is walking around in heaven together with Satan and God asks, "Did you see Job who is a righteous individual?"

Satan responds, "What do you mean, *righteous*. He has everything he wants. Why shouldn't he be *righteous?* He has a big family, a big house, everything."

So God says to him, "Okay, you can take away everything except his life and you'll see he will still remain righteous."

Satan proceeds to destroy Job's family (except his wife) and all his possessions. Job is left sitting alone, suffering and penniless. He begins to mourn and according to the chapters 1, 2 and 42, he never loses his faith.

However, in chapters 3 through 41 he does complain. Who wouldn't? He says, "God! I was good to you all this time and this is what you do to me?"

Job is one of the Jewish answers in those days to the problem of evil. But it is not adequate for us today.

"How is it," says the author of the book, "that God will ordain that a righteous man will suffer while seemingly wicked people prosper?" The discussion of this problem is called theodicy.

Lest you think that I'm being *chutzpadik*, there is a Rabbi in the Talmud who says that Job never existed. In other words, one of our great sages, a long time ago, came to the same conclusion; that an imaginative person wrote the book because he wanted to teach a lesson.

The Book of Ruth

Now let me tell you about the *Book of Ruth*. In Christian Bibles the *Book of Ruth* comes immediately after the *Book of Judges*. It does so because of the opening verse: "And it came to pass when the Judges judged . . ." The people who put together the Christian Bible concluded correctly that the story of Ruth happened during the period of the Judges and so they put it at that particular point.

What is interesting is that as we read those delightful chapters of the *Book of Ruth*, we find that every once in a while the author, writes "That **in those days** this was the custom." This means that in the writer's day it was no longer the custom.

This same writing technique can be found in the *Book of Genesis*. One little verse snuck into the *Book of Genesis* has the phrase: "the Canaanite **was then** in the land." When the author wrote, "and the Canaanite **was then** in the land," it must mean that the Canaanites were no longer in the land when the book was written. It is clear that this part was put in by someone who lived hundreds of years after Abraham when the Canaanites were gone from the land.

But to get back to the *Book of Ruth,* what the author tells is a fascinating story. A Jewish man marries a Jewish woman who bears him two sons. The family leaves their home in Bethlehem and moves to the land of Moab. The two sons get married, each to a Moabite woman. Then the two sons die before they have offspring. The father himself dies.

There is a dead giveaway as to what is going to happen to these characters. The author of the book is brilliant. He calls the two sons *Mahlon* and *Kilion.* A *"choleh"* is a sick one. A *"kilion"* is a finished one. Would anybody in his right mind call his sons "sickly" and "finished?" But since the author is going to have them die before they have offspring, he calls them *Mahlon* and *Kilion.* Each person in the *Book of Ruth* has a name true to the character.

So this woman, Naomi, who has lost her husband and two sons decides to return home to Bethlehem. And she says to her daughter-in-laws, "You should stay with your Moabite people. Besides, I'm too old to have any more children."

In those days when there was the marriage of a woman and the husband died before the woman bore him a son, the brother of the dead male was supposed to marry his widow in order to carry forward the name of the original husband. These were known as *levirate* marriages. If

Naomi had another son, he would be obligated to marry the two sisters-in-law.

One of the daughters turns her back and goes home. Her name is Orpah which means *the back of one's neck.* Again, the character plays out his/her name.

The other daughter, Ruth who is a faithful woman, says to her mother-in-law, "Ask me not to leave you."

> *"Whither thou goest, I will go.*
> *Where thou lodgest, I will lodge.*
> *Where thou dieth, I will die.*
> *Thy people shall be my people.*
> *Thy God shall by my God . . . "*

Naomi says to Ruth, "Okay, come back with me."

Ruth and Naomi travel to Bethlehem and they meet a man named Boaz. Boaz translates to *in him there is strength,* which means he is going to be a valiant, decent human being. Boaz winds up marrying Ruth.

At the end of this short story is a list of their descendants, down to the fourth generation with includes our great King David. That is all and the story ends.

The author's goal was to tell a story without stating the moral lesson which is that sometimes it isn't so bad to marry outside our faith if the non-Jew becomes part of the faith and produces children who follow our traditions.

If the author stated this directly it would have been against the majority opinion in the Bible. The *Book of Ezra*, specifically, says, "Put away your foreign wives." The *Book of Ruth* tells of a difference of opinion on a moral issue. The author wrote the most idealistic book imaginable showing a different point of view.

I think the *Book of Ruth* is also a *bubba mayse.* It is a story invented a thousand years later than the time of the Judges to disagree with the teachings of Ezra. Ezra said that foreign women are not good as wives for Jewish men. Our writer wanted to say, "not always."

It is to the credit of our early Rabbis that they were smart enough to include the *Book of Ruth* when they put together the Bible. They understood that intermarriage depends on the individual and how the individual acts.

The Book of Esther

With all the historians trying to find the King Ahasuerus in the *Book of Esther* and the festival of Purim, they have never been successful in identifying him among historical Persian rulers. Chances are that the *Book of Esther* is also a made-up story.

We teach it to our children because this made-up story is truer than most real stories. Unfortunately there are many countries in which the Jews lived and in which some Haman, Hitler—whoever it might be—says:

> There are a certain people in this land whose laws are different from the laws of the king, neither do they keep the king's laws.

This is the classic example of the half-truth: that the Jewish laws are different, right; but that we don't keep the king's laws? Wrong! Jewish tradition and the Talmud say that the law of the land is the law that the Jew should observe.

There are parts of the *Book of Esther* that are universally true and have been true throughout Jewish history. Not being able to finger who the king really was didn't stop it from being a great story. There is no corroborative evidence as to who Mordecai was, nor that there was an Esther. Does it matter? Does it make the story less effective? Does it make the Bible any less true or beautiful?

The Hebrew Bible and Its Unique Laws

The Hebrew Bible is the greatest book ever written and the greatest Jewish contribution to civilization. I believe the Bible is a human document, written by humans over a long period of time. Some stories are totally fanciful, yet true in their greater intent to teach.

In the *Five Books of Moses*, where we have a tremendous amount of insignificant laws about building a sanctuary, we also have a law that states, "If a person is walking on the street and sees a mother bird sitting on eggs about to be hatched and the person wants to enjoy the eggs for a meal, the person must first drive away the mother bird, then he may eat the eggs." Here we see the humaneness and the sensitivity of Jewish law, especially compared to almost all other legal systems.

If the mother bird were to see the individual eat its eggs, it would cause her stress. The Bible wants the Jew to be sensitive, even to a mother bird. It is that sensitivity that makes us Jews what we are and we get it from our Bible and its lessons.

Our Bible also has a Law that says, "If the ox of your enemy is fallen you should surely raise it with him."

Listen to what it says: You should raise it *with* him. If the ox of your enemy is fallen and he doesn't want to raise it, then you are not responsible. He has the prime responsibility. If he tries, you must help, even though he is your enemy.

Conclusions

I believe that the Bible is the word of humans inspired by God. And I think that sometimes humans today know more than the most inspired people who lived in Biblical days. After all, they were the products of their times. If there are wise men today who proclaim that a particular concept of our day supercedes what is written in the Bible, the assumption is that they have enough evidence and knowledge, and have enough gumption and ethical feeling to come to that conclusion.

I believe the Bible is the starting point for morality, not the last word. When any religious authority, Jewish, Islamic or Christian, turns to the Holy Scriptures and says that this is the way it is because it is written in scripture, I see that as a medieval idea. We have gotten beyond the Bible, Koran, and the New Testament. They are the cornerstones and the starting off points but we have to move beyond Biblical teachings to confront many of today's ethical issues. Religion has to be a stepping-stone to the advancement of civilization and not a cement-block that weighs us down.

✡

Chapter Three
God and the Modern Jew

I AM AN ECLECTIC, ONE WHO GATHERS FROM VARIOUS SOURCES to develop his or her own personal philosophy. The purpose of this description of Jewish belief is to try to make you eclectic, too, because we will discover that on any subject whatsoever, there will be such a wide variety of Jewish beliefs, that we can't possibly label any philosophy as "the" Jewish belief.

In the course of our discussion I will borrow from Mordecai Kaplan, Martin Buber, the *Hassidim.* I will borrow from Jewish mysticism, Jewish philosophy, and whatever source I can to arrive at my beliefs. You may borrow things that I don't, and I may borrow things that you don't. There is a wide variety of Jewish beliefs, not only about God but about life and death, about many other subjects.

Judaism today is a wide enough tent to include all of us. I advocate that:

1. Each of us comes to conclusions based upon knowledge.

2. We shed our childish beliefs.

Note: I am indebted to Rabbis Rifat Sosino and Daniel B. Syme for some of the background material in this chapter. See their book *"Finding God."*

The greatest danger to Jewish continuity is that most Jews in America say they are either atheists or agnostics. They are reacting against what they learned when they were children. We have gone so far beyond what we believed when we were children that to still think that way is a formula for disappointment, disillusionment and eventually defection.

Cults pick up Jewish youngsters who are vulnerable at college age. Every time I trace the background of a Jewish youngster that has been grabbed by the cultists, it is usually a youngster without a good Jewish background, who is rebelling against a childish notion of God. He/she never achieved an adult level of understanding of Judaism.

Look at our current disappointment with *Bar/Bat Mitzvah*, when a youngster, instead of celebrating his/her coming of age, thinks he or she is celebrating a festival of freedom—freedom from Jewish learning and from Jewish thought.

This constitutes one of the greatest threats to Jewish continuity that we have today. In all of our studies we have come to the conclusion that the Jew who goes to school up until the age of thirteen and leaves after *Bar Mitzvah* may be a thing of beauty but, too often, is forever gone— a *goy* forever.

Many Gods

The Bible says, "God is One," but in the earlier parts of the Bible, God is not the only God—not even according to our Hebrew Bible. We sing a song *mi kamocha, baelim Adonai.* This translates to: "Who is like you among the **gods**, O Lord."

What is this business, *among the gods?* Didn't it ever raise your eyebrows? Why do the Jews sing "Who is like you *amongst the gods,* O Lord?"

Jewish thinkers have concluded that even in the days of King David, (1000 B.C.E.) Jews believed that our God was the **One God** but that other people had their gods. And the proof text of that is from one of the stories of Kings Saul and David in the *First Book of Samuel.*

Saul was king before David. Because he was a mighty warrior, David became his general and a rival of King Saul. When David came back from battles, the people would proclaim that Saul had slain thousands but David had slain tens of thousands. No king likes to hear his general is better than he is. So, according to the Bible, Saul became jealous and eventually wound up pursuing David. David has to run away to that present day trouble-spot called Gaza . He goes to the king of the Philistines.

Eventually David tried to move back to the land that Saul dominated only to be pursued again. In a very visual scene Saul stood on one mountain and David on another. David yelled across at Saul, "Why are you chasing after me. What did I do to you?"

Saul gave a feeble excuse, then, David charged Saul as follows: "You forced me to run away from the land of my God to a land of the Philistine's god." Now David is the most God-intoxicated poet of the Bible, yet David believed that while God was the God of the land of Israel, the Phillistine god was the god of land of Philistines.

This is an example in our Bible of the progression from the idea of one God who is the God of Israel while other kingdoms had their gods, to a later idea of One God with no other gods possible.

Henotheism is the term modern scholars have given for the belief in one God who is superior to all other gods, which is what David believed. While David believed in one God, that God was not yet the God of all the world.

Two Gods

There was another philosophy originating in Persia called Zoroastrianism that taught the belief that there were two gods. There was the God of good and the God of evil. In many ways it explained away a subject that troubled the believer in one God: How to explain a good God permitting evil?

When Judaism encountered Zoroastrianism, probably during the Babylonian exile (600 B.C.E.), some found it was an easier explanation of reality. There was a good God, the God of light and there was a bad God, the God of darkness, constantly struggling with each other. If the God of light won out then there would be a good conclusion, but if the God of darkness won out then there would be a bad conclusion. So, to many, the most natural explanation would seem to be the Zoroastrian one.

One God

But up spoke our prophet Isaiah. By his time Jews were monotheistic and believed that there was only one God. Isaiah said, "You are the God who created both good and evil." From that day to the present we, who believe in one God, have to struggle with the question that if there is only one God, why does God permit evil and suffering—especially the suffering of the innocent?

If we are to believe in one God, and God is responsible for everything, we have to ask how God permits the death of infants, or earthquakes and other natural catastrophes that take away innocent people? We eventually have to ask how God permitted such a monstrous movement as Nazism that led to the extermination of six million of our people.

From the Jewish point of view, it is much more complicated to believe in one God than to have two gods. Nevertheless, for the Jew, while it is harder, it is the only way.

God's Appearance

Strangely enough, with all the talk about God in the Hebrew Bible, there is not one description of what God looks like, or for that matter, *is* like. The Biblical texts put the question very strangely. *Moses* was told by God, "Come up to this mountain where there is a burning bush and *experience* God.

There, *Moses* said to God, "God, tell me who you are."

And God said to *Moses,* "You can not see my face but I will make all my Goodness pass before you."

God is saying that in the Jewish faith we will never arrive at a description of what God *is.* The most we can determine is what God *does.* We cannot "see God's face." We can attempt to explain what God does. Throughout Judaism's development, from the days of Moses to the present, we will not find any description of God.

The God of History

In the Jewish way of thinking beginning with our Bible, God is the God of history. When we read the story of the Exodus, it wasn't *Moses* who led us out of Egypt. God led us out. God used the instrumentality of *Moses* to accomplish the task. To emphasize this point, when we celebrate Passover, we do not see *Moses'* name mentioned in the traditional *Haggadah* because the credit for taking the Jews out of Eygpt belongs to God.

Immediately after the defeat of Saddam Hussein in the Gulf War, I said in a sermon: "I still believe in the God of history but not in the same manner as most Orthodox Jews who believe that God interferes in every-day events. I believe God so set conditions in motion that, in the long run, the good will win out."

I had urged that we go to war against Saddam Hussein. When asked how a Rabbi can stand on the pulpit and encourage war, I said I did so because I believe that if we expect God to save America, Kuwait or even Israel from the onslaught of a tyrant, without human instrumentality, it will not happen. My philosophy is that God guides history, but not with a heavy hand. As the story of the *Exodus* reads, "It was the finger of God."

The Chosen People

The Bible teaches that Jews are the *Chosen People—Chosen People,* yes, but not any better. We are a people chosen for a particular purpose. I believe that purpose is to teach morality to the world. No people, not even today, is as driven by morality as the Jewish people.

Show me one other people that is willing to return territory it won in war at the cost of the blood of its sons and daughters. And yet, most Jews believe that for Jews to dominate another people is morally wrong. So the land is given back.

The moral imperative is that Jews, if we are to survive, have to live a just life. This moral imperative has pursued us from our beginnings up to today. In that respect, we are a *Chosen People.*

Our Covenant with God

From the beginning, and from "the beginning" means from Abraham's time, God made a covenant (or a pact or a treaty) with us, God on one side and Israel on the other. Those who understand law know that any kind of a contract needs what is called "consideration" — I have to do something for you and you have to do something for me.

Judaism believes that if we are to be true to the Covenant, we have to observe God's law. The Orthodox believe the "law" means the minutiae of Jewish practice. Reform Jews believe that we have to observe God's law in the ethical sphere. That is our duty. If we will do that then God will observe God's part of that pact, namely God will see to it that we will continue to exist.

Let me put it in the reverse—in the negative. If we do not observe God's law and we break the Covenant, why should God see to it that we survive? If we, as Jews, are going to be like all other people, then we should be subject to the same historical laws as other nations.

In our Bible we have this covenantal relationship and even to this day in the Modern period some Jewish thinkers believe that if American Jewry is to continue to exist, we will have to go back to what is called **covenant theology,** the belief in the treaty between God and the Jews, each doing something for the other. In the process, the Jew also knows we haven't been so observant of our part of the bargain.

If God were only a God of Justice, every time we fell short, we should have been punished, perhaps until we would no longer exist. Fortunately, God also is compassionate.

But if God were only a God of Compassion, then we could get away with doing whatever we wished.

So many modern Jews, and I among them, believe that God is at one and the same time, a God of justice and a God of compassion, which is a teaching as old as the Bible.

A Personal God

God, to the Biblical Jew, was personal. Every character of note in the Bible had a personal relationship to God. Everybody talked to God. Everybody knew that God was watching. God wasn't a remote God, who only created the universe and let it run on its own. God is a God who is involved in the life of the individual if the individual wants to relate to God. There was the possibility of personal involvement with God in the Bible and that personal involvement was available to every individual, great or small.

How then do we explain a good God who permits suffering? The Bible was unable to give an anwer. It tried various alternatives but in the end the Bible says that there are certain things that the human does not know and we have to be satisfied that our minds are finite and we cannot understand everything. We can't really understand why people suffer or why evil sometimes thrives on earth.

The Talmud and God

The Talmud, which is a further explanation of the Bible, also makes a contribution to our understanding of God. The Talmud accepts that there is only one God, not one God amongst other Gods. There are no other Gods in the Talmud.

If we see a house, it implies that there had to be a builder of the house. The house didn't get put together by itself. Rabbi Akiva, (100 C.E.) one of the great Rabbis of the Talmudic Period, said that since we see this universe, isn't it therefore implied that the universe needed some thing, some spirit to put it together? The creation of the universe implies a Creator.

Angels as God's Helpers

But the Talmud added (and this is something I do not believe in) that since God had so many things to do, God needed some messengers. The messengers of God, which are hinted at in the Bible, are really elaborated on in the Talmud. This is where the influence of Babylonian culture affected the Rabbis of the Talmud.

These messengers of God in the Talmud were the angels. Angelology in the Bible was rather elaborate. However, we should note that all the angels in the Talmudic period, and even in the beginnings of the Bible, were subject to God.

Justice and Mercy

The same idea of God's judgement introduced in the Bible is elaborated in the Talmud. God has the attribute of justice and the attribute of mercy. If God were to run the universe with one and without the other, then the world could not exist. It is only when justice and mercy are combined that God permits the world to continue.

The special bond between Israel and God in the Talmud was further developed by traditional Judaism, and this special bond becomes so precious that the way the Jews follow our part of the Covenant is to observe the interpretations of Jewish Law as our Rabbis explain them. When the Talmud said, "Observe the *mitzvot*," it was stating how Jews could live up to our part of the Covenant.

The Bible said we should not do any manner of work on Shabbat. The Talmud asked, "What is work?" It then gave "forty-less-one" categories of work." It listed all the things that we are not allowed to do on Shabbat; sewing, tearing, cutting, building, etc. The Talmud said that for the Covenant to be fulfilled by our half of this treaty, the Jew has to observe all of these Laws.

Now, interestingly enough, the Talmud also taught, "We do not know what God is and our knowledge of God is limited. But, God is close to whoever calls on God." In other words, if we really want God in our lives, God will become close to us. That theme was repeated much later by *Hassidism* (1800 C.E.) and by many of the contemporary movements in Judaism.

Sin and Evil

But where the Talmud went further than the Bible, is that the Talmud tried to explain why there was sin or evil in the world. It said, "If people suffer, then it must be because of one of three reasons:

1. I may not admit, or even know, that I did something wrong but my suffering is God's punishment for what He knows that I did that was wrong;

2. Sometimes I am beginning to skirt the edge of goodness and my suffering is a good warning to me that I better be very careful;

3. We really do not know why we suffer. Human understanding is limited. We found this thought first in the Bible itself.

A Medieval Jewish philosopher gave us the following illustration:

A young boy was once on the beach with a pail in his hand and a philosopher was watching him. The young boy took the pail, ran into the ocean, filled the pail with ocean water, ran onto the beach and poured the water out.

The philosopher turned to the young boy and said, "Young man, what are you doing?"

He replied, "I am slowly emptying the ocean waters onto the beach."

So the philosopher laughed and said, "In that little pail, he is going to empty the ocean waters?" And then he said, "But am I not trying to do the same thing with my limited mind, (limited pail). I am trying to figure out all that there is to know about God? Like the little boy, I have such a limited understanding. I cannot possibly empty the ocean into my own mind."

Furthermore, the philosoher said, "Everything that I see has a cause. If a boat is out in the ocean, the reason is that somebody gave it the power to go out into the ocean. But there had to be the first cause, the One who caused the event the first time."

That first cause is what the philosopher called the "unmoveable mover." God was the first mover but God Himself is unmoveable. That first cause is God.

Our philosophers introduced this thought into Judaism. They used their minds to try to explain, not what God *is*, but everything that we can learn about the *experience* of God. The medieval philosophers are mostly "rational philosophers." They used their reason to try to explain their belief in God, and gave us logical proofs for the existence of God.

My Own Personal Beliefs

It is now appropriate to give my own personal beliefs about God, which are eclectic, yet follow the Jewish rational philosophers.

I believe the God created the universe and today lets it run mostly by itself, according to the laws of nature. God has also built into these laws of nature a moral spirit so that good eventually triumphs over evil and, for Jews, *mitzvot* lead to the betterment of the human condition.

Hitler and Nazism had eventually to be defeated. Natural catastrophes will occur and sometimes good people will perish together with evil ones.

I pray to God to give me strength and courage to do my life's work. God can be my partner in working out my personal and my people's destiny. But God, by Himself, will not act without the human's participation and cannot be expected to fulfill the wishes of any person or any people.

God and Jewish tradition are the sources of Jewish idealism. I participate in worship services to connect me with that Jewish idealism. Sometimes Jewish idealism has to be altered to accomodate contemporary thinking and knowledge, especially as it relates to Jewish law.

(My personal beliefs about God are further elucidated in Chapter Eight.)

✡

(l. to r.) Fred Plotkin, Rabbi Zeldin, Abe Hershenson, on site of Stephen S. Wise Temple, 1967

Rabbi Isaiah Zeldin
of
Stepeh S. Wise Temple (l.)
with
Uri Herscher (r.)
then student at
Hebrew Union College
1966

(l. to r.) Rabbi Isaiah Zeldin, Rabbi Mordecai Kaplan with Norman Eichberg and Ben Winters, first two elected presidents of Stephen S. Wise Temple, 1966

Rabbi Isaiah Zeldin
and
Stephen S. Wise Temple
Educational Director
Metuka Benjamin
1990

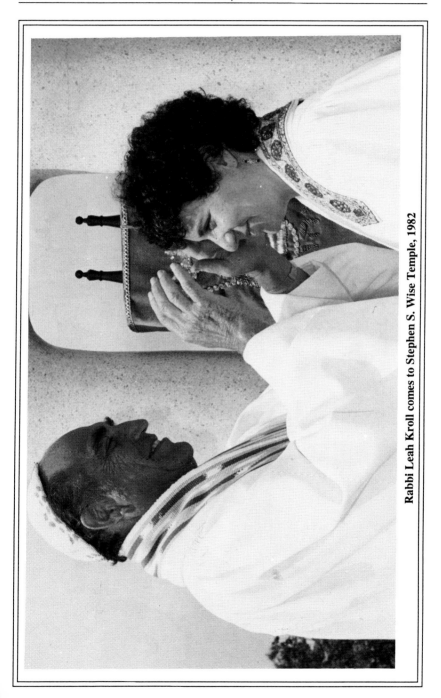

Rabbi Leah Kroll comes to Stephen S. Wise Temple, 1982

The Honorable Jean Kirkpatrick,
United States Representative
to the United Nations
and
Rabbi Isaiah Zeldin
1991

The Honorable Madelyn Allbright,
United States Representative
to the United Nations
and
Rabbi Isaiah Zeldin
1993

(top, l. to r.) Dr. Michael Zeldin, Rabbi Leah Kroll, Joel Zeldin, Karen Zeldin (bottom) Florence Zeldin and Rabbi Isaiah Zeldin, 1990

Chapter Four

The Evolution of Jewish Law
3,500 Years of Change

HALACHAH MEANS JEWISH LAW. It comes from the Hebrew word that means "to walk." In Judaism the Law tells us how we are supposed "to walk;" how we are supposed to live our lives.

The general understanding is that *Halacha* came from Mt. Sinai, where most Jews believe that God gave at least the Ten Commandments to Moses. Othodox Jews believe that God gave the entire Torah to Moses there on Mt. Sinai. The approximate year was 1300 BCE or three thousand, three hundred years ago.

In the Torah, especially in the *Book of Exodus*, there are many laws. The origin of Jewish Law to the Orthodox, or traditional Jew, is through Moses from God Himself. This is an extremely important concept to bear in mind.

The Five Sisters and the Flexible Torah

There is a story in the *Book of Numbers*, about five sisters coming to Moses in the desert and saying, "We know that under Jewish Law property passes from a father to his sons. We also know that the land is to be divided in the Promised Land we are about to enter. Our father has died. We are women. There are no sons in our family. May we have our father's inheritance?"

The Torah says that Moses didn't know the proper answer, so he inquired of God. God said the women were correct. If an inheritance were to stay within the confines of the family for whom it was originally intended, then even though Torah Law says that a man must inherit property from his father, in this case, the daughters should inherit.

This story is in the Torah without any embellishments and without drawing the moral lesson. These five women appeared before Moses saying that they knew what the Law was but they believed the primary intent of the Law was to maintain inheritance of families.

Implied here is that the Law is flexible because it can be interpreted according to newer circumstances. In other words, Jewish Law lends itself to updating. In this case Moses had two principles in conflict.

1. Inheritance belongs to the sons of the father.

2. An inheritance must remain within the realm of that particular family.

The Torah teaches that with each new situation we have to weigh the pros and cons and make a decision that is more in keeping with the intent rather than the letter of the Law. The Torah does not actually say this outright. Had it done so, Jewish law would have been a lot more flexible in the ages that followed.

The Static Torah

We read in the first sentence of *Ethics of the Fathers* in the Talmud (200-500 C.E.), that Moses received the Law from God and gave it to Joshua, his disciple. Joshua taught it to the elders, the elders to the prophets, the prophets to the men of the Great Assembly and from then on to the Rabbis. According to tradition, Jewish Law was taught from Moses in 1300 B.C.E. up to the time that the Talmud was written down (500 C.E.). To the traditional Jew, Jewish Law is mostly a static continuum of teachings from the time of Moses all the way to the Talmud, and even to later ages.

The Changing Torah

It is my viewpoint that traditional Judaism, contrary to what many believe, has been in a constant state of flux and change since the days of Moses. Modern scholarship shows that the Torah was not even known by the people, let alone practiced, until about the year 600 B.C.E. or from six to seven hundred years after Moses.

The Rediscovered Torah

In the *Book of Kings* our Bible relate that King Josiah (600 B.C.E.) discovered a copy of the Torah. This is the first time since Moses that there was any reference to the Torah itself. History teaches that while the teachings of Moses were being handed down by word of mouth from teacher to disciple, the people themselves had little or no idea about it. It was not until another two hundred years passed that Ezra the Scribe (400 B.C.E.) ordered the Torah to be read, for the first time, to the people. This was another two hundred years after the rediscovery of the Torah scrolls.

The People's Torah

It is only when we get to the year 100 B.C.E. or three hundred years later that we begin to hear of ordinary people who are knowledgeable about the Torah. By then there were *yeshivot* and academies. We had Rabbis, teachers and students, and the dissemination of Jewish Law had become widespread. This indicates to scholars that from the days of Moses, for a thousand years, the knowledge of Torah was maintained only by a select few. Of special note is that by the time the Talmud was finally written down, (500 C.E.) some Torah Laws had been so reinterpreted, that entirely new practices had become part of what was then considered traditional Judaism.

The Expanded Torah

There is one verse in the *Torah of Moses* that reads *"thou shalt not seethe a kid in its mother's milk."* That's all there is in the entire Torah about mixing of milk and meat.

Does this mean that the prohibition against mixing milk and meat was not known in Moses' day? From a modern scholarly point of view, it was neither known nor practiced in those times. The separation of milk and meat was a development after Ezra (400 B.C.E.).

Two Points of View

Orhodox Judaism says that when God gave the Torah to Moses (1300 B.C.E.), He also explained to Moses all of the later Laws that were eventually written down in the Talmud (500 C.E.). This is called the *Oral Law*. Moses then taught it to Joshua and Joshua taught it to the elders and the elders to the prophets, etc.

There is the great difference of opinion as to where Jewish Law originates. To the Orthodox, the *Halachah,* including all the later rulings, was originally taught by God to Moses at Sinai. To the modern Jewish scholar, Jewish Law developed, as needed, through the generations.

A Modern Viewpoint

Reform Rabbis love to tell the story about Rabbi Akiba, (100 C.E.) one of the most influential Rabbis who organized the Talmud into its six different orders and major sections. This story is in the Talmud, but I tell it in modern words:

> Moses, a thousand years after he was up in heaven, says to God, "God, I worked so hard to bring the Torah to the children of Israel, are they still observing it?"

> God replied, "Well, I'll tell you Moses, you don't have to take my word for it. Go down and see whether the children of Israel are studying the *Torah of Moses.*"

> So Moses wound up in a classroom of Rabbi Akiba. When it came to the interpretation of Jewish Law and tradition, he took different letters, different words, and implied suggestions of the Torah and gave them interpretations that were entirely new.

> Now Moses was in Rabbi Akiba's classroom. Moses sat in the back and listened to the lecture. He didn't understand a thing. He went back and said to God, "I heard Rabbi Akiba explaining the *Torah of Moses* and I didn't understand him."

> "God asked Moses, "Were you satisfied that your Torah was being studied even a thousand years later?"

> Moses thought awhile and said, "Yes I was."

The Talmud, by this story, teaches that even though Moses himself did not understand the later interpretations of his original teachings, the mere fact that his Torah was still being studied, albeit in a new way, satisfied him enough for him to say that his Torah was still alive.

This, actually, is the viewpoint of Reform Judaism, many Conservative Rabbis as well as other knowledgeable people. We believe that Jewish Law continually developed from the time of Moses on through the 1700-1800 years to the period of the Talmud, and even later.

Changes

All Orthodox Rabbis admit that there were times when Jewish Law had to be changed. If a prominent Rabbi made the changes and was recognized by everybody as an expert, then his rulings became the new Jewish Law.

One of the most prominent Talmudic changes had to do with a law regarding debts. Debts, according to Jewish Law, were supposed to be cancelled every seventh year. In the Torah the purpose was to make it easier for the debtor to survive. If a poor man had to borrow money in the second or third year of a cycle, and still couldn't pay it back in the seventh year, the Torah didn't want him to remain poverty stricken all his life. So the Jewish Law in the Torah was that every seven years all debts were cancelled.

Twelve hundred years later, Hillel, (100 B.C.E.) one of our great teachers prior to the *Mishna* (Talmudic Period) said that the very Law that was supposed to help poor people was now working against them. By the time the fourth or fifth year of the seven year cycle, no lender wanted to lend money to the poor, knowing that in two or three years the debtor would not have to pay back the loan. A poor man who needed a loan found himself unable to borrow money.

So Hillel instituted a legal fiction. He ruled that the court was not subject to this Torah Law. Therefore, during the seventh year—the Sabbatical Year— the person who owed the money had to pay it back, not to the lender, but to the court. The court would then pay the money to the lender. This simple device, or legal fiction, made it possible for a poor man to borrow money at a time when he would otherwise be denied.

A Process of Growth

To Reform and Conservative Jews there has always been a process of growth, adaptation and even subtraction in Jewish Law. There is a whole system in which edicts are promulgated by prominent Rabbis who are recognized as authorities. The Rabbi basically proclaims that because of a particular situation, Jewish Law doesn't work. So he changes it.

Up until 1000 C.E. Jews were permitted to have as many as four wives, just as Moslems and Bedouins are today. That year Rabbi Gershom, an Ashkenazi Rabbi, recognized as an outstanding authority, promulgated one of these rulings. He announced that henceforth in the Ashkenazi community, a Jewish man could have only one wife. What helped to make this change in Jewish Law acceptable was that among Ashkenazi Jews it was already the general practice to have only one wife. Since there were only exceptional cases where someone had two or more wives, the ruling of this highly respected Rabbi was immediately accepted.

However Jewish Law tried to be fair with its changes. It was understood that if a person, at the time of the new law, already was doing a certain thing, it usually didn't undo what he was already doing. We know this today as a *grandfather clause.*

In 1948 a number of Yemenite Jews who had two wives, immigrated to Israel. Israel has a *Law of Monogamy* for Jewish families. That year the Knesset decided that if a Yemenite immigrated to Israel with two wives, he could keep them. But if a Yemenite settled in Israel, and then wanted a second wife, that was illegal.

Decision by Vote

Jewish Law has aways been adaptable. The Talmud (100-500 C.E.) shows that when a question of Jewish Law was debated in the *Sanhedrin,* the Rabbis first argued the case. When the debate was finished, they usually took a vote. The majority prevailed and the majority opinion became the Law.

The Talmud tells a fascinating story of a student asking a great sage why, when he had one point of view and against him there was a majority, he still maintained his point of view, but when his student questioned him on this issue he gave the point of view of the majority. The Rabbi responded that when he held his own point of view it was because he had learned it from his teachers. How-

ever, at that time they had not taken a vote on the matter,
The Law was not yet decided. But, since his students
heard it from him after the vote had been taken, his point
of view was no longer valid and the student must follow
the majority. The Jewish rule of law was that the opinion
of the majority of recognized sages rules.

This principle of law, once we have majority and minority opinions already questions the belief that Jewish
Law came from Moses. When I was a student, I did a
paper on Rabbi Sherira Gaon who lived in Babylonia
around the year 1000 C.E. He wrote on the development
of Jewish Law. His students questioned that if God gave
the Law to Moses and Moses gave it to Joshua and so on,
why are there are often two opinions as to what is the
Law? He responded that, unfortunately, at a certain time
before there was the School of Hillel and the School of
Shammai, the students didn't learn from their teachers
as well as they should have. So some of the Law became
confused. Since no one knew what the exact Law was,
from that point on, Jewish Law followed the majority
opinion of the sages.

God-Given or by the Majority?

Once it was decided that Jewish Law was to follow the
majority then it is clear to any logical mind that the claim
that it is God-given Law is no longer valid. Humans now
made the final decisions as to what the Law was. And if
humans made the final decision, we should not, at the
same time claim that this was God's Law. At best it was
God-inspired.

The Orthodox argument that Jewish Law really came from God to Moses and was transmitted by the chain of tradition, is self-contradictory.

The Practice of the People

Hillel and Shammai (100 B.C.E.) were the two great teachers in the generations before Rabbi Akiba. The Talmud tells how a person ran up to Hillel and asked, "What kind of knife should I use to slaughter an animal?"

Hillel replies, "I don't remember. Go to a certain town. In that town the people are very meticulous in their observance of slaughtering animals. You will see how they do it and you will know that that is the Law."

There is another concept in Jewish Law that if the Law says one thing, while the people practice otherwise, the custom supercedes the Law.

As a modern parallel, we have jaywalking laws in Los Angeles. If I cross a street in the middle of the block I may well get a ticket and be fined. In New York they also have jaywalking laws. Three years ago a New York policeman ticketed somebody for jaywalking. When it came to court the judge threw it out, saying that the custom (of jaywalking) supercedes the written law (against jaywalking).

Unanswered Questions

In the years of the Talmud, decisions of the Rabbis of the *Sanhedrin* became official Jewish Law because they were decided by the majority. But every once in a while the *Sanhedrin* didn't make a decision. Sometimes the Talmud gives two opinions but doesn't decide the Law. It never took a vote. Eventually the Talmud was completed, (500 C.E.) comprising sixty-three volumes which make up the interpretations of what is in the *Torah of Moses* (1300 B.C.E.). However, we still had those problem areas where no decision had been made. Also, we had new situations not covered by Jewish Law.

Responsa Literature

After 500 C.E. Rabbis themselves often wrote to the heads of the most prominent Rabbinic academies of that generation in order to solve problems left unanswered in the Talmud. From the year 500 C.E. to the year 1000 C.E., the heads of three of the Rabbinic institutions in Babylonia were considered the most prominent sages. They would reply with what they considered to be the correct answers to the questions asked.

This type of expansion of Jewish Law is called Questions and Answers, and its writing is called *Responsa* Literature. The questions themselves were written by Rabbis from outlying areas such as North Africa, Spain, or Southern Europe.

We have a prayerbook from the year 900 C.E. as part of this Question and Answers procedure. A Rabbi wrote asking the proper order of prayers. He received an answer that wasn't a prayerbook, just the first word or two of each prayer. His teacher knew that the Rabbi asking the question could fill in the rest.

This type of *Responsa* has continued on to the present. During the World War II there was a committee of American Rabbis set up by the Jewish Welfare Board to answer the specific questions of American servicemen in unique situations.

A kosher-observant serviceman asked if he was allowed to eat the food at mess since the government didn't serve kosher meals. The board responded that since he was serving in the armed forces in an emergency situation, and since not eating would make his chances of not surviving even greater, he may eat the general mess food. Generally the answer also had reservations. In this case it was that he should try to refrain from pork products and shellfish.

Reform *Responsa*

We have current *responsa* literature in the Reform Movement. What if there is a non-Jewish husband and a Jewish wife who have decided to raise their child in the Jewish faith, and the child is going to become a Bar Mitzvah. In what ways can the non-Jewish husband participate in the service of a Reform temple?

This is not a question in a Conservative congregation because the Conservative Movement still rules that Jewish Law is valid in all of its implications. Therefore only a Jew can participate in a *minyan* and the synagogue service.

There are currently at least two dozen books of Reform *Responsa* and there must be an equal number of Conservative *Responsa*.

The Continuing Evolution of Jewish Law

It is clear that we had a systemization of Jewish law around the year 500 C.E. when the Talmud was completed. This took place only fifteen hundred years ago. From 500 C.E. to 1000 C.E. we had **Reponsa** that were kept privately by various Rabbis. Around the year 1000 C.E. the Babylonian academies ceased to be the main centers of Jewish learning and thought. Jewish academies in Spain, North Africa and Europe came to the forefront for the next five hundred years.

In Spain there were three great Rabbis who decided that since they had all these *Responsa* it was time to gather them together and write them down as codes of Jewish Law. Once again, Jewish Laws were systematized, written down and put in one place. There were three different compilers, each with his own Code of Jewish Law; Isaac ben Jacob Alfasi (1100 C.E.), Moses Maimonides, (1200 C.E.), and Jacob ben Asher, (1300 C.E.).

The Code of Jewish Law

A great Sephardic Rabbi named Joseph Karo (1600 C.E.) took the works of these three great scholars and created the *Shulkhan Arukh, The Prepared Table.* Since he understood the tradition that Jewish Law follows the majority, he consulted the three sources and whenever two outvoted one, that became the Law. To this day, his work is recognized as the authoritative Code of Jewish *Law* on the subjects that it covers.

Karo wrote this *Code* for Sephardic Jews. A German Rabbi reviewed the *Code* and said that Ashkenazi Jews practiced Jewish Law differently. He took the four volumes of Karo's *Code* and wherever an Ashkenazi practice was different, he wrote in the margins, "This is not so. We do such and such." Although he intended to criticize the authority of Joseph Karo he actually made the *Code* the authoritative book for both Sephardic and Ashkenazi Jews with the understanding that Ashkenazi Jews follow the marginal notes.

"Sealed in Cement"

The problem with the *Code* is that it put into writing many answers to questions that were still open to additional interpretations. Joseph Karo preserved Jewish Law for future generations, and for that everybody is grateful. But at the same time he made it almost impossible for Jewish Law to do what it had always been doing, namely, adjusting to circumstances, conditions and newer interpretations. So the very thing that preserved Judaism in the sixteenth century also threatened Judaism because it ceased evolving.

Reform Judaism as a Response

That is why Reform Judaism developed 200 years later. By the time we got to 1800 C.E., many Jews were becoming modernized, especially in Western Europe. These modern Jews looked at the *Code* and saw it as medieval while they were entering the Modern Period.

And so, almost with one fell-swoop, first the lay people and then Reform Rabbis said that Jewish Law was no longer valid. They also took many of the ritual practices of Judaism and decided that since they no longer accepted Jewish Law, they would also eliminate many traditional Jewish practices. What practices to keep and what practices to eliminate has been a dilemma for Reform Judaism for almost 200 years.

Perhaps a Mistake?

In the Spring of 1995, the retiring head of the Hebrew Union College, Dr. Alfred Gottschalk delivered a paper at a Rabbinic convention stating that he believed that Reform Judaism made a mistake when it threw out *halachah*, Jewish Law.

The basic differences between the three major Jewish movements today is each one's view of Jewish Law.

Orthodox Jews have to observe Jewish Law as it was given by God to Moses, down the chain of tradition to the *Code of Jewish Law*, with a few adjustments since then.

The Conservative movement follows the same path as the Orthodox, except that it says that it has to find ways to bring Jewish law up to modern times. But until it gets around to changing the Jewish Law and until the change is properly accepted, the current Jewish Law is to be observed by Conservative Jews.

Reform Jews say Jewish Law is no longer valid. We will study it. We will try to get at the spirit of Jewish Law but we will not observe the letter of the Law. Or as one great preacher put it, "We will give Jewish Law a vote, but not a veto."

Now the president of the Hebrew Union College—the Reform Seminary—believes we made a mistake when we threw out Jewish Law.

His statement inspired me to examine Jewish Law that has to do with questions that are vital to so many Reform Jews.

Jewish Divorce-*The Get*

In Jewish Law, the woman as well as the man can initiate conversation about a divorce, but the woman has to have the consent of the man so that the final action of the divorce can take place. The man however, doesn't need the consent of the woman. This inequality already invalidates Jewish Law as a guiding principle on the subject of divorce to a modern Reform Jew.

There is a whole tractate (volume) of the Talmud called *gittin*—divorces. This tractate was based upon the idea that it was a man's world. Since the man was the dominant party in a family relationship, the man initiated the divorce and arranged for the divorce ceremony. This is not today's world and hence Jewish Law causes all kinds of problems.

For example, if a married man disappears and there are not two witnesses to say he died, then according to Jewish Law, his wife remains married. She can not re-marry. But if a woman disappears the husband writes a bill of divorce which goes through the Rabbinic court and the man becomes officially divorced. He can legally take a new wife.

Israel operates all lifecycle matters under strict Jewish Law. Since the man must consent to a divorce there are a lot of women who can't get divorces because their husbands blackmail them, asking for huge settlements. So Israeli Rabbis have methods to put pressure on a husband when they see this injustice. They might go to the husband's employer and ask that unless the husband grants the divorce, he be fired. In some cases the husband goes to jail rather than give a divorce and even the Rabbis are powerless under their interpretation of Jewish Law.

According to Jewish Law, there is such a thing as a *conditional divorce*. An Israeli soldier going into battle may write a *conditional divorce* and give it to his wife or a Rabbinic authority. The *conditional divorce* states that should he be missing in action, then the wife is permitted to use this *conditional divorce* as if he divorced her before he went into battle. Therefore the wife would be able to remarry if he were to be lost without witnesses.

Surprisingly enough, the Jewish Theological Seminary's law committee now writes a *conditional divorce* to be attached to every Conservative wedding in case the husband disappears or refuses to give a *get* in the process of getting a divorce.

The modern Jew looking at all of this often asks who needs all these *shenanigans*. Since everybody knows that I am probably the most traditional of the Reform Rabbis in Los Angeles, I constantly get phone calls from Conservative colleagues because a son or daughter of an important member of that congregation has gotten divorced without a Jewish *get* and now wants to remarry. Conservative Rabbis, who are required to adhere to Jewish Law cannot perform the wedding. But they don't want to lose the family as members, so they call me and ask me to do the wedding. They know that I will not use the wedding to attract the new couple away from the family's synagogue to my congregation.

Conservative Jewry is now in a crisis because of Jewish Law. Almost every Conservative publication has articles about the crisis and disillusionment in Conservative Judaism, because every survey shows, that while the Rabbi is supposed to adhere to Jewish Law in a Conservative congregation, the overwhelming majority of the members are much looser in their practices.

The Reform Dilemma

Now look at the dilemma we have as Reform Jews. We know that our Reform Movement threw out Jewish Law and thought that Judaism was only ethics. We believed we had to practice goodness but could forget Jewish ceremonies. We downplayed Hebrew and many Jewish practices. We so watered down Judaism that our rates of intermarriage soared. They are higher than the Conservative Movement whose own intermarriage rates are higher than the Orthodox.

The Reform Movement has come to the conclusion that eliminating Jewish Law entirely was a mistake. Yet here is our dilemma. We could go back and say that Jewish Law is valid, but we have to change it. Unfortunately, the changes don't come nearly as rapidly as the times demand. But for the Reform Movement to give up why it is "reform" would also be a mistake.

Suggestive Reform

In the past thirty or so years there has been a movement in Reform that has advocated publishing guides to Jewish practice. Jewish Law says that during Passover I cannot take unleavened foods into my house. A Jewish guide would say it is *suggested* that during Passover I use only *matzah* in my house. It is *suggested* I light candles on Shabbat, and that I have *kiddush,* that I say *Hamotzi* over the *challah,* and that I have some kind of Jewish observance with the family for Shabbat.

Practice versus Abstract

The Reform movement has come to the realization that Judaism can not be taught in the abstract. Rabbis cannot ask their congregants to teach their children to *feel* Jewish, or to be a good person. This doesn't preserve Judaism. What preserves Judaism is a person's conscious involvement in Jewish practices during the entire year.

Unless Jewish families observe Jewish holidays, unless they observe Shabbat in some fashion, unless they belong to and attend a synagogue and give their children a Jewish education, they can't preserve Judaism for future generations.

Reform Judaism now believes that it would like something that has the effect of Law but not the strictness of traditional Jewish Law. How to do that is both the biggest dilemma and the biggest challenge we face as Reform Jews.

Survival: Based on Freedom or Law

All the statistics seem to indicate that in the future less than 10% of American Jewry will be Orthodox and in Israel less than 20%. Despite all we hear of the *Baal Teshuva,* (one who returns), and of the Aish Hatorah, Young Israel and Chabad movements, all the surveys show that same 10% or less of American Jews being Orthodox. We cannot turn back the clock. An American Jew lives in a free society. A free society is a society of choice. In too many aspects of Jewish and American life, Orthodoxy is wanting and can't bring itself to change.

The Conservative movement has the crisis of Jewish Law supposedly changing, but not changing nearly fast enough for its followers. The result is that there is very little difference in practice between the members of most Conservative and Reform synagogues. There is a difference among the Rabbis, but not in the membership.

Overwhelmingly, I think the percentage is about 55% of the third and fourth generation American Jews prefer Reform—but for negative reasons. Reform is the least demanding.

Many people want to be Jewish. Ask the average American Jew if he or she wants to be Jewish? Judaism has become the "in" thing to be; much different then it was fifty, forty or thirty years ago. But most Jews are not doing enough about it.

Reform leaders have come to the conclusion that the only way that Judaism can be preserved is through ritual practices and ceremonies, with some form of sanctions behind it. Can we continue to say to our people, "Yes you can be Jewish. You should have *matzah* in your house on Passover, but if you don't, we'll understand?" It is not enough to say whatever a person decides is okay.

When we threw out Jewish Law we made a mistake. We should have been more discerning and we should have kept some of the strictures of Jewish Law. On the other hand, we reject Orthodox Jewish Law, nor can we adhere to the Conservative philosophy.

This is our dilemma. Now it's time for us to think of a solution—or, at least, to propose one.

Intent

Reform Judaism is much more interested in the intent rather then the letter of the Law. However, once we go to the intent, we still have to make a decision. And this is where the rub lies.

I recently officiated at the funeral of one of the members of our congregation. She had a stroke. The doctors did a carotid artery operation and then her husband, also a doctor, looked at the post-operative X-rays and saw that her brain was essentially gone. He asked the attending physician to remove her from life support and let her expire. The attending doctor said that if he did that he would be in trouble with the hospital. So the husband-doctor replied that he would be the responsible doctor. She died a minute or two after they took her off life support.

I looked into what Jewish Law would have to say about this situation and found it against the hastening of death of another person. However, there is no prescription that says that one must prolong the life of an individual beyond the point where there is any meaning to that person's life. In other words, Jewish Law supported what the husband had done. He didn't inject air in her veins so she would die quicker. He did nothing to hasten her death. All he did was take off the "artificial" life-support system so that she died naturally. His intent was correct.

Abortion

Reform and Conservative Judaism have consistent positions on abortion, namely that the woman has a right to make her own decision. However, some Rabbis are of the opinion that it should not be an unlimited right. Even a Reform Rabbi looking at Jewish Law could come to the conclusion that abortion in the third trimester might be going too far. According to Jewish Law, the child is not an individual until birth. If a child dies up to thirty days after birth, we don't formally bury, we don't have a funeral ceremony, and we don't sit *shiva.*

Through the years I have officiated at funerals of infants who died in the first week or two of life. I have done so, seemingly contrary to Jewish Law, because I have a conflict with two sets of Jewish values. There is a principle of the Talmud that says that certain things may be done even if contrary to Jewish Law, to preserve peace.

In one particular case, a mother carried the baby for nine months and had already picked out a name and furnished a room. That baby was a presence in that family's home even though the baby died. For me to have told the woman that Jewish Law says the baby was not yet a person would have been cruel. Therefore, I officiated. My intent was *the way of peace.*

The Role of Non-Jews in Services

Let me go back to a question that I raised that is perplexing regarding the participation of non-Jews in services, especially at B'nai Mitzvah in Reform congregations.

The problem is when the mother has not converted to Judaism. Remember, Reform Judaism changed the traditional Law to say that if the child of a Jewish father and a non-Jewish mother is raised Jewish, then the child shall be considered Jewish. What should I do if on the eve of the child's Bar Mitzvah, the non-Jewish mother comes to synagogue and expects to light the Shabbat candles on the pulpit? She's brought the youngster to Jewish day school for the past five or six years. She knows that all the other mothers of B'nai Mitzvah are lighting the candles from the pulpit on Friday night. Her relatives are there and she says she wants to participate.

What she is asking is contrary to traditional Jewish Law. But I have to ask myself, as a Reform Rabbi, "What is the moral and ethical intent? What is the higher principle?"

Conclusion

I have come to the conclusion that in most cases I will accomodate to the personal needs of member families. I have two requirements when confronted by difficult questions:

1. Is it good for the future of the Jewish people in America?

2. Is the request of the person asking me to accomodate an honest request or made only for appearance sake?

I will thus officiate at the intermarriage of a child of a member, if, after several meetings with the couple, I am convinced that should there be children, they will be raised in the Jewish faith.

I will permit non-Jews to participate in Bar/Bat Mitzvah services, but not in parts that are strictly Jewish, such as being called to the Torah.

I will counsel with families on life and death issues and support them in difficult decisions as a friend and as a representative of Jewish thinking, but without imposing Jewish Law on them.

While in extenuating circumstances I might also help non-affiliated families, I reserve most of my services to member families—not because of exclusivity, but rather because I have ongoing relationships with member families and the after-effects of my ministrations are observable and adjustable.

Jewish Law, to me, is an instrumentality aiding the preservation of our people. Where it hinders our preservation by being obtuse, or even worse, is in sharp conflict with modern sensitivities, I will disregard the Law and follow my conscience. But I would like to revive the spirit and intent of Jewish Law and believe that sometime in the future, Reform guidelines will take hold among our congregants, not with rigidity, but with loving acceptance.

To some of my learned Reform friends, that will occur, say they skeptically, the day after the Messiah arrives.

✡

Chapter Five
Jewish Ideas of Messiah

ONE OF MODERN JUDAISM'S most delicate and difficult subjects is the idea of the *Messiah.*

A mother sent her son out to get a job. At the end of the day he came back and she said, "Nu. So what kind of job did you get?"

He said, "Well, first I went to the market and they offered me a job as a boxboy for fifty cents an hour."

She said, "Did you take it.?"

He said, "No."

She asked, "Why not?"

He continued, "Because I went across the street to the other market and they offered me a different job. I would have to carry the packages out to the car and there I would get tips. They offered me thirty-five cents an hour with tips."

She said, "Did you take it?"

"No. I saw an old Jew standing on the corner and he offered me an even better job."

So she said, "What was that?"

He said, "Well, he wanted me to stand on the corner and wait for the *Messiah* to come."

"And how much did he offer you?"

He said, "He offered me twenty-five cents an hour."

"Did you take that?"

"Yes," he said, "I know that the pay isn't good but the work is steady."

This insightful Jewish joke is a lead-in to a subject that has caused Jews more anguish than any other subject in the course of our long history—the concept of *messiah*. Like so many other subjects, when we discuss the Jewish idea of a *messiah*, we have to consider what period of time in Jewish history we are discussing.

Messiah

My first twelve years as a Rabbi, I was a professor. I would often lecture on the Jewish ideas of *messiah*. It is a troubling area because Jews are accused of being the deniers of who the Christian world considers to be the *Messiah*.

The words *Christ* and the word *Christian* means "those who believe in the *messiah*." *Christ* is a Greek word which translates in the Hebrew to *messiah*.

The Jewish Concept of Messiah

Messiah first appears in the Hebrew Bible as an entirely different concept than most would imagine. In earlier Biblical literature the translation is " to anoint," or more specifically, "to pour." A prophet would take a special vial of oil and pour it over the head of whoever was to be the "anointed one" and then that person was king. In other religions a high priest often "anointed" a new king.

King David, the Annointed One

King David is the most visible, significant and popular individual in the Bible who was "anointed." David is seen as the ideal king in the Bible, not because he was a flawless individual, but because he was God-intoxicated.

David was the sweet singer of God. David was a poet as well as a warrior. He is reputed to be the author of the *Book of Psalms*, a series of writings that praise God. Perhaps he didn't write them all but he certainly started that type of literature. He was the ideal king even though when we read the *Books of Samuel* we see that David was a most human character.

The phrase "anointed of the Lord" refers essentially to David. Later, in Talmudic times, when Jews began to look for a new "anointed one," he was expected to be descended from the house of David.

When we hear the expression *Messiah ben David,* it is a way of saying that this is the *messiah* that the Orthodox Jew expects. He is of the house of David, the same human David who was "anointed," sinned and nevertheless was not rejected by God.

In no place in the Hebrew Bible is there direct reference to an individual *messiah,* except for one who is "anointed" to be a human king or a ruler.

Two of the rather minor prophets, Micah and Zechariah, speak about the time when they hoped that an "anointed one" would come and be king over the Jews once again. They even name the person that they expected to be the "anointed one," a man named Zarububal who would lead

Jews back to Jerusalem after their exile in Babylonia (400 B.C.E.).

In the Book of Daniel there is a side reference to some kind of *messianic* idea. In one sentence it says, "And those that sleep in the dust will be raised to life again." Most modern scholars see this as a metaphor for Israel.

The Prophets and the Messianic Age

Our prophets speak of a *Messianic Age*—a time in which all the troubles that the Jewish people were undergoing would be eliminated. In our Bible there are various views as to what this *Messianic Age* would be. When Jews were oppressed and especially after the destruction of the First Temple, they hoped that a time would come when the scattered people would be gathered together again back in *Eretz Yisrael,* our Holy Land.

The Messianic Age and Redemption

Our prophets teach:

1. When I do wrong, I am sinning;

2. If I sin, I will be punished;

3. I will be given a chance to repent;

4. From repentance comes redemption.

In most of the early period of Jewish history there was little need for the Messiah because we had our own land. In the period before the destruction of the First Temple the prophets warned our people that if we sinned, we would be punished.

Later, we were punished. Our Holy Temple was destroyed and we were exiled to Babylonia. Then the prophets added the other two elements: we would have a chance to repent, and there would be redemption.

What I have said so far is not complete. Some of the prophets who lived in the year 750 B.C.E., before the destruction of the First Temple, said that if we did not repent, there would be no redemption. We were sinning and the punishment had not yet taken place. That is how we got the popular misconception of the prophet as one who foresaw the future, saying that in the far future our country would be destroyed.

An anonymous prophet in the *Book of Isaiah* said, "The people have sinned. They haven't been punished and they are continuing to sin. I look forward in the far distant future for a period when there will be peace on earth and each man will dwell under his vine and under his fig tree and none shall make him afraid."

The prophecies that talked of the distant future were prophecies that had to do with the *Messianic Age.* But these prophecies were not about an individual *messiah.* The idea of an individual *messiah* is mostly absent from our Hebrew Bible.

There are a couple of passages in the *Book of Isaiah,* (chapters 11 and 53), where it speaks of a time when a child will lead the people, the lion and the wolf will dwell together in harmony, and an individual will be beaten for the sins of humankind.

All Jewish Biblical scholars and most Christian scholars, agree that even though these passages are written in the singular, the phrases had nothing to do with an individual. The Jewish people were suffering because of the sins of mankind, and Israel would be the suffering servant, paying for the sins of humanity.

The writings of our Hebrew Bible were completed by the year 200 B.C.E. An additional group of fourteen writings were later put into a little book called the *Apocrypha*. That little book, in which incidentally we have the *Book of Maccabees* with the story of Hanukah, contains no mention of an individual *messiah.*

After the time of the *Apocrypha*, and before the destruction of the Second Temple in the year 70 C.E., there was a style of literature in the *Apocryphal* mode. It is only here that we see the beginning of the idea of an individual *messiah.* From this literature the new Christians picked up the idea of Messiah, especially due to the terrible conditions of the time.

False Individual Messiahs

Through the ages we have had many people who were either thought to be, or claimed to be, the *Messiah.* In each instance, his followers suffered. In some cases, it almost destroyed Judaism in the area where the so-called *messiah* lived.

One such pseudo-*messiah* was such a marvelous charlatan that he convinced the Pope that he was the *Messiah.* He predicted an earthquake and the earthquake took place so the Pope actually believed he was the *Messiah.* Eventually he met his fate like all other pseudo-*messiahs.* He was killed.

Between 1650 and 1800 C.E. we had two prominent pseudo-*messiahs,* Shabbetai Zevi and Jacob Franks. These two led hosts of people away from Judaism.

Throughout the last two thousand years, there have always been prominent Rabbis who supported the idea that a *messiah* is necessary to save the Jews from their oppressors. At the same time we had other prominent Rabbis who warned against the idea. A Talmudic passage tells:

> If you are planting a tree and you hear somebody shout that *Messiah* is out on the street, first finish planting, then go see if the *Messiah* is there.

The Jewish communities that followed the false *messiahs* committed some of the greatest follies imaginable. One of these pseudo-*messiahs* sent word to his followers that he would soon take them all to the Promised Land. They sold their property at one tenth its value, got up on their roofs, and waited for the *Messiah.* When he didn't come, they got down from their roofs and were homeless because they had squandered all their possessions. Unfortunately, this has been a recurring event in Jewish life.

Modern Messianic Ideas

There were two people who wrote great books on the Jewish *messiah* idea. One, Joseph Klausner, a generation ago, was from Israel. He was, perhaps, the greatest Biblical and post-Biblical scholar of his time. His is a very technical book but students of Judaism delight in his depth of scholarship.

The second one who traced all the false *messiahs* from the days of the Talmud to the present, was a leading political activist in the Zionist movement. His name was Rabbi Abba Hillel Silver, a great preacher.

The Reform Movement

The Reform movement came on the scene around 1800, less than two hundred years ago. Its philosophy said that Reform Jews don't believe in supernaturalism. God doesn't suspend the forces of nature to do anything that the human is unwilling to do for himself or herself.

One of the first things the early Reform leaders concluded was that we no longer believe in an individual *messiah*. But since they knew that the *messiah* idea was so ingrained in Jewish thought, they took from the Hebrew Bible all those magnificent writings of the *Messianic Age* when there would be peace in the world, when we would love one another, when there would be enough for all, and when neighbor would not fight against neighbor. They called this the *Messianic Age* just as our Bible did.

Reform Judaism said that rather than wait for an individual *messiah* to bring about this remarkable period in time, each individual, each Jew, should contribute towards bringing the *Messianic Age* closer to reality. The idea of the *Messianic Age* instead of an individual *messiah* is now one of the cardinal principles of the Reform Movement.

Zionism

Differing from the *Messianic Age* hope, is another concept introduced by the Zionist Movement. Zionists believed that many of the troubles of the Jewish people came about because we had accepted the fact that we should be oppressed, and simply waiting for God to send a *messiah* only increases our troubles.

The Zionist Movement concluded that instead of hoping or praying for a *Messianic Age,* Jews should do in the first place what the *Messiah* was supposed to do: gather the Jewish people back to *Eretz Yisrael* and establish our homeland again. Then Jewish destiny would no longer depend upon the goodwill of our often resentful host countries, but upon ourselves.

Although the Reform Movement and the Zionist Movement rejected the idea of an individual *messiah,* until fifty years ago, they were opposed to one another.

The Reform Movement believed that Jews should work in the country in which they lived to further freedom and equality. The *Messianic Age* will come about when the Jew is accepted as an equal in whatever country he/she lives. Reform Jews didn't look forward to the time when Jews would be gathered together in one place, even if it was the Promised Land.

As a matter of fact, early Reform leaders reinterpreted Jewish history. They said Jews had mourned the destruction of the Second Temple and Jerusalem in the year 70 C.E. but that that event turned out to be a good thing. Jews were scattered and in whatever land we resided, we became the teachers of religion and morality to the rest of the world.

The only problem with this doctrine is that we suffered at the hands of tyrants and leaders of other nations and religions for hundreds of years. When Hitler came along, a number of countries became *Juden frie*—free of Jews. The supposed teacher of religion was put to death because it was the teacher who really highlighted what the tyrant wanted to destroy.

My father had a theory of the lion and the lion tamer. When the lion is under the watchful eye of the lion tamer, the lion controls himself. But if the lion should break away and the lion tamer can no longer control him it is the lion tamer that the lion attacks first.

My father believed that Hitler turned on the Jews because Hitler understood that if he was going to conquer and oppress the nations of the world, he could not succeed while the "tamers of civilization," the Jews who brought values to civilization, were still around. Therefore, Hitler first picked on the Jews and nearly destroyed them.

Modern Day Miracles

I believe sometimes it is good to believe in the impossible. When a person prays for Grandma to get well and Grandma dies, instead of coming to the conclusion that either God didn't listen or Grandma was inadequate, or the prayers for Grandma were faulty, we have to conclude that nature has run its course. I have preached this doctrine for a long time in the following way:

> Who is the better watchmaker? Is it the one who makes a watch and has to improve it every day, to tinker with it, and adjust it? Or, is it the watchmaker who makes the watch and lets it run by itself?

I believe the second is the better watchmaker. I think that the God in whom I believe is the better Creator for first creating a watch and then not tampering with His laws of the way it operates. It is for this reason I don't believe in supernatural miracles.

I believe in miracles. I believe it is a miracle when I see a baby born, and I count ten fingers. But I don't believe in a miracle which is the suspension of the natural order of events. God did not stop the bullet that was headed for Yitzhak Rabin. God does not protect the soldier on the battlefield who is in the line of a machine gun. There are certain events that just take place, which is the way nature works. That's the way I believe God made it to work.

Rabbi Harold Schulweis in his new book wrote, "God is not a noun but rather a verb." He advises that what we should believe in is "Godliness." Just as justice is Godly, so we should do justly.

One of the most moving prayers on the High Holy Days is *"Hear our voice, O God."* We hope that somewhere there is a Being able to respond to each individual, even though it might be sometimes "yes" and sometimes "no."

I have had doctors tell me that a person is going to die in six weeks yet fourteen years later that person is still alive. The active Spirit of the human being that is the mystery of human existence, I call God—a noun, not a verb.

Similarly, there is a time when the *Messiah* as an idea is very helpful. Of the Jews in the concentration camps who faced obliteration, most who remained alive were Jews who believed. Victor Frankel's *Man's Search for Meaning* demonstrates that those Jews who believed had a better chance of survival because their life had meaning.

The most popular song that came out of the concentration camp is about belief in the *Messiah—Ani ma'amin*, *"And even though He tarries, I still believe."*

There comes a moment in life when the situation is so full of anguish, that there is no way out. At those times it is good to believe that somehow, miraculously we will be saved, even though it will not happen most of the time.

Having said that, to make belief in a *Messiah* a prominent part of contemporary faith would undermine the effort for self-fulfillment and individual effort to better the human condition and the Jewish condition in the world. Therefore I deemphasize the *Messiah* idea and leave out preaching about the *Messianic Age.*

A Chosen People, A Unique People

I believe that we are a *Chosen People,* a unique people. This doesn't deprive any other people of thinking that they are also a unique people. We are a unique people, that is taught to confront life in a special way. The journey itself, to Jews, is most important. And along that journey we must accord other peoples the right to travel their own ways, yet helping those who are unable to make their way in the world.

I believe that Jews should live the way God wants us to live. We ought to live in the finest ethical way possible. When, in Biblical literature, it says that we should be a "light unto the nations," then if the nations want to learn from us, fine, well and good. And if they don't, that is fine too. But I believe that we ought to strive to do that which is right. We ought to try as individuals and as a people to live as an exemplary people.

An exemplary people is different from saying that I want the rest of the world to convert to my faith or recognize my mission.

The Christian Messiah and Anti-Semitism

Christianity took our idea of *messiah* and changed it from an idea of a human being to a deity. No subject has caused more distress and more persecution for Jews. For centuries Jews were looked down upon for being the deniers of what the the Christian world accepted as the *Messiah*.

Christmas in the old country was when our people were accused of being "Christ killers." Late in his life, my father suffered a stroke. We were going to a wedding and I wanted him to get dressed early. He said to me, "We can't go, it is a Sunday."

I said, "So what about Sunday?"

He said, "The anti-Semites will be out looking for us."

His mind went back to Russia where on Sundays and all religious holidays for that matter, Jews were open game. He played cards all night on Christmas eve, not in disrespect for Christianity, but to be awake in case anti-Semites attacked.

Except in a class, I never use the word "Christ." I say *Jesus. Jesus* was born a Jew and died a Jew. The theology about *Jesus* was written after his death, mostly by Paul, who never met him.

I have no objection to *Jesus*. But I do have strong objection to the word *Chri*st which means *Messiah*. *Jesus* as *Messiah* means to me something other than what I know *messiah* to be.

In Jewish tradition, the *Messiah* was first and foremost a political individual. Jesus is said to have said, "Render onto Caesar that which is Caesar's and render under God that which is God's." That is like saying, "Let us not mix in politics." I happen not to agree with that philosophy. It definitely is not Jewish!

Now you understand why it is so important for Jews to understand the Jewish concept of *messiah*. When somebody rings your doorbell and wants to sell you a Christian Bible that shows that the Bible is fulfillment of prophecy in the "Old Testament," you should know how to respond. Unless you know the answers and unless you teach your children the answers, Judaism is in danger of disappearing as a religion.

Whoever thought that the time would come in America when the Jew would be accepted as we are today? There is hardly a Christian family that doesn't have somebody in it who is intermarried with a Jew. They usually discover that the Jew is really a fine person. But whoever thought that when things would be so good for Jews, it would be so bad for Judaism?

Good Times, Bad Times

When times are bad for Jews, everybody rallies to the cause. When times are good for Jews, as they are now, we tend to quietly disappear, to assimilate. We assimilate because many of us do not know the beliefs of the Jewish faith.

American Jewry is the most educated of all groups in our society. We are more privileged in America than even the Episcopalians, and the Episcopalians are the blue-blood Americans most represented in *Who's-Who*. We outstrip Episcopalians in most fields of endeavor. We are really the "Episcopalians" of America.

But our prosperity threatens to be our undoing. We circumcise and we Bar Mitzvah and we have marvelous parties celebrating these events.

Teaching at a Mature Age

But we don't seriously discuss Jewish ideas with our thirteen-year-olds. We only discuss these concepts with older teenagers when they are mature enough. That is why we established a high school—so we could communicate Jewish ideas and beliefs to more older teenagers.

The other day I visited first the 7th and 8th grades, and then the 9-12th grades of our high school. The 7-8th graders put on skits about the Rabbis of the Talmudic period and what these great sages taught. It saddened me to realize that what these children know of the Talmud is greater than the knowledge of 98% of my congregants. For forty-five minutes in a Judaic class, without a note in front of them, the students acted out a complete chapter of the *Ethics of the Fathers* from the Talmud.

Then I went into a 12th grade class in Jewish philosophy where they were taking up Maimonides' view of the *rodef*—the pursuer—with all its various arguments, especially as it was wrongfully applied by the assassin of the Israeli Prime Minister.

Conclusion

Perhaps it is fitting that I conclude this chapter on the *Messiah* with a plug for Jewish education, especially on the high school level. We would have no need to worry about the inroads made on Jewish youth by the cults, nor the harm done us by anti-Semites or those who condemn us for not accepting the Christian *messiah*. If more of our older teen-agers, and our college youth as well, would study Jewish beliefs they would know how to answer those who think that our Bible predicted a *messiah.*

I rather hope that the battle for the Jewish soul, while ongoing, will yet lead us to a higher plane of Jewish knowledge.

✡

Chapter Six
The Jewish Soul and Prayer

A NUMBER OF YEARS AGO, when Israeli soldiers were still patrolling the Gaza Strip and the West Bank, ultra-liberal Jews were saying that Israel, by controlling a people that do not want to be dominated, was losing its "soul." They decided that it was the most effective way to put forth their political agenda. They believed that putting it in moral terms made a better political argument. They invented the idea of a "group" soul.

Body & Soul

At the time, I thought this was an effrontery, because they said nothing about the Arab penchant to justify terrorism and were silent about the Moslem soul. Besides, if we preserve the Jewish soul, but there are no Jewish bodies in which to preserve the soul, there will no longer be any Jewish souls.

The origin of *"we are losing our soul,"* comes from a Jewish teaching that the individual is a combination of two elements: body and soul. Our body, says Jewish tradition, comes from the earth while our soul comes from God. In a living person, body and soul are interconnected.

When it comes to "body and soul," the Jewish teachings on these subjects are mostly found in the Talmud. The Talmud uses Biblical thoughts and then develops them further.

The Rabbis of the Talmudic period integrated the idea that our body comes from the earth, while our soul comes from heaven. This Talmudic quote defines the soul:

> As the Holy One, blessed be He [meaning God], fills the whole world, so the soul fills the whole body.
>
> As the Holy One, blessed be He, sees what cannot be seen, so the soul sees but cannot be seen.
>
> As the Holy One, blessed be He, is pure, so the soul is pure.
>
> As the Holy One dwells in the innermost parts of the universe, so the soul dwells in the innermost parts of the body.

The soul cannot be seen, which in modern terms is saying that we cannot prove that we have a soul, just as we cannot prove that there is a God. We can only theorize that we have a soul. When a Jew dies, we recite a prayer that comes from the Rabbi's manual based upon an early verse in *Genesis (3:19):*

> The body returns to the earth as it was and the soul returns unto God who gave it.

This is a primary Jewish belief and has been so without change since the times of the Talmud. Therefore, we can say that Jews have believed in the soul for about two thousand years.

A Parable

> Once there was a king who had many servants. One day he said to them, "I will give you clean fresh garments. I want you to preserve them as much as you can."

There were some foolish servants. Whenever they had to do any work, they worked in their new garments. They soiled them, they dirtied them and when they were finished they gave them back to the king.

There were also some wise servants. When they had to work in their special garments, they cleansed them. They refrained from dirty work in those garments because they knew they had to return them to the king.

This parable teaches that God gives us a soul that came to us pure or "clean." And when we are no longer on the face of the earth, we are expected to return that soul as clean as when God gave it to us.

Elements of Jewish Soul

The most common Hebrew words for soul are *nefesh, ruach* and *nishama.*

Nefesh is the blood or the element that flows through the individual. It is our vitality. But, even in the Talmudic teaching, *nefesh* ceased at death because what flowed through an individual, stopped when the individual was no longer alive.

Early in our Bible it says God created man, "And He breathed into him, *Ruach Elohim*—the spirit of God." When we are born, God breaths into us a *ruach,* a spirit. It is that *ruach,* the spirit of God, that is in each of us that is expected to be returned to God, as pure as possible, when we are no longer alive.

The same is true of the *nishama.* In Yiddish, we say *"er hut a zisse nishame*—He has a sweet soul."

It is the cultivation of the soul that is really the prime challenge to the individual.

When I meet you as an individual, I see your physical appearance, but I don't know what your soul is like. I don't know what kind of a person you really are. I don't know what your values are, what your worth is. Your soul, that I don't know and that I cannot see, exists just as much as your physical attributes. That soul, your *nishama*, is what life is all about. The cultivation of each person's *nishama* is essentially the challenge of human existence.

So we have to ask, "At which point in the birth of a human being is the *nishama* breathed into the individual?"

A Talmudic story.

Rabbi Judah, who was the editor of the *Mishna*, had a discussion with a Roman. The Roman asked the questions, "Does the soul enter the human at conception or at birth?"

"Can a soul remain 'unsalted' and not go bad," asked the Roman, "if the soul enters the human at conception? It is unsalted. It is unflavored. Therefore, it will go bad by the time it is born."

So Judah thought and then said to his students, "The Roman taught me a great lesson. It shall be Jewish teaching that the soul enters the body at birth and not at conception."

This is an important concept when we discuss the Jewish view on abortion.

Source of the Soul

The Talmud gives an answer as to where the soul originates. I am not quite sure that we, today, would accept the

Talmudic answer. Strangely enough, Plato and the Greek philosophers are in accord.

Said they, "Somewhere in the seventh heaven is a storehouse of souls." In other words, God has reserved a special "storeroom" and every time a birth takes place, He takes one of the souls and puts it into the newly born baby.

While my scientific mind rejects the idea of a seventh heaven, the idea of the soul coming from God has become part of me. I do not speculate where my body goes after I die—whether it goes to a heaven or a hell; but I still believe that the soul returns to God who gave it.

If, when a person is born, each of us is given a soul. then God is wise enough to know where that soul should return.

I believe that there is a spiritual force in the human being. That spiritual force within each human I call the "soul."

Psychiatrists know that there is some kind of a force within the individual. They call it the psyche. I picked up a book just a few weeks ago by a friend who was a chaplain in the Second World War and then went to medical school and become a psychiatrist. He wrote a book, *From Soul to Psyche.*

I read his book and discovered, in his two professions, he was dealing with the same thing. When he was a Rabbi, he called it a soul. Now that he is a psychiatrist, he calls it a psyche.

The Highest Challenge

I believe the cultivation of the soul is the highest challenge to the individual. Nothing is more meaningful to a human being. It is the self-worth of each individual. It is the significance of each person's life.

This challenge is what inspires us to high ideals. It is what prompts us to do what is good and to reject what is bad. It is what our entire Torah is all about.

The Torah doesn't dwell on what we should do to our bodies but it does talk to us about what we should do to our souls. It tells us how we must cultivate elements of our inner being.

When Jews are bidden to observe the Shabbat, the purpose of observence is because (in Talmudic tradition) on Shabbat each Jew is given an additional soul. This is the day when we are supposed to spend time, not on material things, not in the pursuit of idle pleasures, but on the cultivation of our souls. God gave us the Shabbat in order to give us a new *nefesh,* a new soul.

I believe that American Jews will not survive as secular Jews, if they do not cultivate their souls. The reason that a religious Jew believes in the soul is to give life meaning. Without the soul there is no significance—no worth to life.

At High Holiday services we listen to messages about *teshuvah*—repentance. We learn that we can damage our soul but we are given a chance to repair it. We can ask for forgiveness and reconstitute it. We can cleanse our soul. This is the message of the High Holiday prayer book.

Creed & Deed

Notice the difference between the Jewish belief and the Christian belief. The soul in the Jewish religion comes pure at birth. The Christian belief is that the soul is born in sin. The way a Christian is redeemed is by believing in *Jesus*.

But in Judaism, we are born with a pure soul. If we sin, we can repent by correcting our misdeeds. Judaism is a deed oriented religion.

Some people say, "Christianity is a religion of creed while Judaism is a religion of deed." While we emphasize the deed, it is based upon our creed. Our approach is that one's beliefs influence one's actions, but in the final analysis it is the deed that counts.

The Real Purpose of Prayer

Many people think that prayer is essentially a petition to God. The reason that most Jews don't pray is that, in the past, when they did pray, they were disillusioned—their prayers weren't granted.

But only one type of prayer is petition. To me, that it is the lowest form of prayer. If I ask God to do what I want and it doesn't happen, can I deduce that there is no God?

Atheists are born out of this naive belief in God. Someone's grandmother was sick and he prayed to God that she would get well. She died. Out went the belief in God.

To me, prayer is an appeal to one's soul to become something better than it was before the prayer was uttered. In other words, the prayer is to make the individual a finer person.

What is faith?

My faith is that every human being has a soul, and the goal of life is to cultivate that soul to its finest development. When the time comes for me to leave this earth, I hope to be able to say, "I did the best that I could to make my soul as understanding, as pure, as giving, and as sensitive as I possibly could."

Conclusion

To believe in immortality because some day the individual will stroll about in *heaven,* is well and good for a childish mind. I do believe in immortality, but immortality consists of something worthy that I have done on this earth that will outlive my physical being. I have left institutions and programs on this earth that I have worked for and I have contributed to my people and my society. These will long outlive me here on this earth. This, to me, is real immortality.

Does it do me any good to speculate about going up to *heaven* or down to *hell?* That is not nearly as significant as what life is all about. If my children and grandchildren carry on my values and my congregants remain devoted to our Jewish heritage—that is immortality enough for me. All the rest I leave to God.

✡

(l. to r.) Rabbi Isaiah Zeldin, Menachem Begin, Sydney Dunitz, Israel, 1969

(l. to r.) Joel Zeldin, Prime Minister Yitzhak Shamir (in his office), Rabbi Isaiah Zeldin, Oren Kroll-Zeldin, Karen Zeldin, 1990

(l. to r.) Rabbi Isaiah Zeldin, Governor and Mrs. Pete Wilson, Florence Zeldin, Lori Milken, 1992

**Rabbi Isaiah Zeldin
and
Shimon Peres,
then Foreign Minister of Israel,
1988**

**Rabbi Isaiah Zeldin
and
Israeli Prime Minister
Yitzhak Rabin
1992**

**King Hussein of Jordan
and
Rabbi Isaiah Zeldin
1995**

Florence Zeldin, President George Bush and Rabbi Isaiah Zeldin, 1991

President "Bill" Clinton and Rabbi Isaiah Zeldin, 1992

Chapter Seven
Live Nobly as if Tomorrow Were to be Your Last Day

ONE OF THE MAGNIFICENT PHRASES in our High Holiday prayer book reads: *Repent one day before your death.* But who knows on what day he/she will die. "Ah," say the Rabbis, "Since you don't know on what day you will die then you are to repent each day as if it was the last on Earth."

I want to turn that phrase around a bit. When I was a young man studying for the Rabbinate, I picked up a Yiddish book that had the High Holiday service in Hebrew on one side and the Yiddish translation on the other. I opened to the front page and read the subtitle, *"fartaitched und farbesert*—translated and improved." I would like to translate and improve the saying *"repent one day before your death,"* to, *"live fully and properly as if tomorrow were to be your last day."*

Life is so tenuous and uncertain and disaster can overtake anybody. There is no such thing as a safe place, not even if you stay at home. So you might as well make the most of the days that you have here and live your days to the fullest and make them meaningful.

Note: I am indebted to Rabbi Daniel Gordis for some of the background material in this chapter.

It is probably a good addendum to live life not only for yourself but for your dear ones as well, because if you live for yourself only, then when you die, you are gone and forgotten. Since we are all here for a very short time, it would be tragic if the day after you are gone no one remembered you. So my addendum to the phrase *"Repent one day before your death,"* is to *"Live nobly each day of your life."*

There is a *halachic* lesson in the Talmud in a seemingly obscure passage in the *Tractate Yoma,* "If a person comes across a recent ruin on the Sabbath and in the ruin he sees a head, is the person allowed to violate the Sabbath by digging?"

I am not going to take you through all the intricacies of the argument but after lengthy discussions in *Yoma* as well as in other texts, the legal decision arrived at is:

> If there is a possibility that the rest of the body whose head you now see visible from the ruin is alive, the saving of a life is more imporant than the keeping of Shabbat. But if it is to recover the body of a dead person, then you must wait until the Shabbat is over, then dig into the ruin to take out the body and to give it a decent burial.

This principal is based on what Jews believe about the preciousness of life. If, to save a life, you have to violate every precept, including Shabbat, you should do so. But once the life is lost then Sabbath becomes more important.

The Sacredness of Life

The concept of the sacredness of life is primary in understanding Jewish Law. If the modern Jew departs from *halacha,* then one should do so only with this concept in mind.

Sometimes I bemoan the fact that in America we really have loyal Jews who like Jewish tradition, who want to remain Jews, and who want their children and grandchildren to remain Jews yet who know so very little about what Judaism teaches on the subjects covered in this chapter. It was emphasized again when I read in the *New York Times* a detailed summary of the Pope's teachings in his edict called *Gospel of Life.* It presents the Catholic viewpoint of life, and does so with scholarship and with sensitivity.

It also implies that anybody who disagrees with any of the Pope's findings is not moral. Judaism starts at the same point that the Pope started his epistle. Judaism agrees with many of his conclusions, but not all. In Judaism there are several possible answers rather than the Papal approach which gives only one.

When we read the Orthodox decisions of great Rabbis of our own day, we see they often differ. A great scholar, Rabbi Jakobovits, who was the Chief Rabbi in England, recently said, "I will tell you what leading Jewish scholars have said on this particular subject and I'll give you both sides of the argument. But please, don't ask me to make the decision."

Now, to have an Orthodox Rabbi know what modern great authorities have decided on delicate subjects and then say he will not tell his opinion is like saying that in certain moral cases there are gray areas that may be decided either way. Having said that I am ready to launch into my beliefs on abortion, birth control, euthanasia, and doctor-assisted suicide.

Birth and Abortion

In Jewish tradition life does not begin at conception. Life begins at birth. Therefore, if we abort a fetus, in Judaism, it is not considered to be murder, since the individual has not yet been born. However, traditional authorities are not pro-abortion.

Why are Orthodox Rabbis against abortion except under certain conditions? In Orthodoxy, the first of the 613 commandments is to be fruitful and multiply. Therefore, it is the highest commandment to reproduce. Abortion interrupts reproduction and is a sin in Orthodox Judaism, except in the case of the *rodef.*

A *rodef* is a pursuer. Some congregations are called *Rodef Shalom*—Pursuers of Peace. The Talmud says, "Be of the disciples of Aaron who loved peace and was a pursuer of peace."

The Torah teaches that killing in self-defense is not murder. If "A" is pursuing "B" and in the process of saving "B" he/she has to kill the pursuer "A," he/she not guilty of murder.

Notice the difference in terminology. We *kill* the pursuer. We haven't *murdered.* There is a world of difference between killing and murdering.

If a thief comes upon me by night *(Book of Exodus)* and is stealing through my window, and if in the process I kill the thief, I am innocent. But if a thief climbs through the window in the daytime, and I kill the thief, I may be guilty of murder. The difference between the two is, in the day time if I yelled out, I might have attracted attention, I might have scared away the thief. It may not have been a risk to my life during daylight if I saw he was unarmed.

But at night I do not know if he is armed or not. And therefore, if I should kill the thief, it is like the *rodef,* the pursuer.

The Exception in Abortion

If the fetus is a *rodef,* that is, if the life of a mother is jeopardized with the possible birth of the new child, it is permissible for an abortion to take place because it is similar to the case of the *rodef.* The fetus is like someone pursuing the life of the mother.

Rabbi Jakobovits says we should have used Jewish legal teachings to influence Israeli legislation on abortion. Had Israel clamped down on abortion, we would have had two million more Jews. Imagine how much more secure Israel would have been if there were two million more native born Israelis.

"But," said he, "The Orthodox Rabbinate, of which I am a part, doesn't permit abortion and if Orthodoxy won't permit abortion, then Israeli practice will ignore Orthodox teachings altogether. As a result, abortions are common-place in Israel. As a percentage of the population abor-tions take place twice as often in Israel as in England."

Motive and Intent

Rabbi Jakobovits wrote that we should not talk about the *time* of abortion, (first trimester, second trimester, etc.)

but we should talk about the *intent* of abortion. By extension of the *rodef*, we also have an answer to someone who was raped. In other words, Jewish law has a way of being lenient when it needs to be lenient and permits abortion in cases such as rape and incest.

So instead of saying abortions are permitted the first or second trimester, let us look at the intent. When the motivation behind abortion is only because it is not the proper time to have children or because economically one can't afford them, we have to consider the effect on the Jewish people which might include bereft Jewish parents who later in life would have wanted another child or two.

One Rabbi at Yeshiva University in Los Angeles wrote that we should not perform ultrasound, because life is sacred and when we teach that life is sacred, who is to say that even a child that is malformed does not have a right to life. Another Rabbi wrote that amniocentesis should be prohibited by Orthodox Jews but ultrasound should be encouraged.

Malformed children discovered through amniocentesis almost always end with abortion. The second authoritative Rabbi explains that sometimes a family that thinks that it wants to abort changes its mind when it hears the heartbeat of a little one and decides to have the baby. Therefore, ultrasound could be used as an encouragement to childbirth.

It is clear that if we were to ask Orthodox Rabbis about vasectomies or tying fallopian tubes, they would all say they were against it. If I had a vasectomy and want it reversed, they would say, "Of course," because it helps me fulfill the first commandment.

In other words, if we start with the assumption that life is desirable and should be encouraged and that the first commandment of the individual is to have a child, then obviously, anything that preserves the sanctity of life should be encouraged.

By that same analogy, if we ask about the new pill RU486, Orthodox Rabbis are against it. They will cite medical authorities against taking the pill. The instances of medical complications of women who have taken the pill are now established. They are not great percentages, but nevertheless, women have had complications from having taken the pill. Some Orthodox doctors say that they do not encourage their patients to take the pill.

Orthodoxy will discuss types of contraceptives. Our sages of the Talmud knew of an intrauterine device, a kind of sponge, almost two thousand years ago. They also knew other birth control methods. Orthodox Rabbis, in certain circumstances, will countenance contraception, whereas the Pope will never countenance artificial devices.

In an age where we have discarded the horse and buggy and don't use kerosene lamps anymore, should we not avail ourselves of modern contraceptive methods? The Pope emphasizes that life should be considered sacred and birth control and abortion make us too callous about life. But the very thing that the Pope tries to teach is undone by too many births that make life unbearable. Orthodoxy also perpetuates Medievalism when it preaches against abortion except in cases of rape or incest.

I do not agree that all cases of mental anguish to the mother are just cause for abortion. I have had a distressful incident of a woman at whose wedding I officiated. One month after the marriage she found herself pregnant and two weeks later discovered her new husband having sex with another woman. She aborted, but she could at least have had a normal healthy baby.

Not so very long ago a woman who had four children unintentionally became pregnant. Her husband, angry at the occurence, said to her that either she abort or he would leave. She aborted and then became mentally ill.

It is distressful to realize that a woman having an abortion in the third trimester does so to a fetus that is formed, has arms, legs, fingers, toes, eyes and ears. An abortion at that point might cause more anguish than having the baby with all the consequences thereafter.

Jewish tradition and the sacredness of life influence me to conclude that not in all instances is abortion justified. I am conflicted by two concerns. One is the right of a woman to make choices regarding her body. The second is the Jewish teaching on the sacredness of life, especially that of a fully formed fetus.

Right-to-Die

Nowhere does the sacredness and dignity of life come into play more than in the area of the right-to-die. The Catholic Church and most *Halachic* authorities agree that passive euthanasia is moral, but we should do nothing actively to hasten the death of a terminal patient. I agree with this general consensus but would go somewhat further and support doctor-assisted suicide in highly regulated circumstances.

If the patient was mentally competent, and had the consent of clergy, doctor and attorney, I would favor doctor-assisted suicide for someone whose suffering was unbearable, with no possibility of cure. The religious teachings of the sacredness of life is enhanced when living without dignity is brought to a merciful end.

Living nobly presupposes living with dignity and all of living aims at being the best we can be in surroundings where the quality of life can bring love, respect and joy to self and family.

✡

Chapter Eight
Conclusions of Fifty Years in the Rabbinate
"God is My Partner"

I WOULD LIKE TO FILL IN SOME OF THE THINGS that can't be said at a dinner or a Friday night service. I begin with my philosophy on the belief in God. I am not a believer in the traditional God. In the Orthodox world in which I was brought up God knew everything and did everything. Omniscience and Omnipresence was part of my Orthodox upbringing.

That illusion was shattered as I lived through the Nazi years as a youngster. It was not possible to continue believing in a God that did everything and knew everything, and reconcile that idea with the fact the six million Jews were systematically being put to death without God doing something about it. To this day, this is the most serious dilemma that believing Jews face. If God does everything and knows everything, how could He have permitted the Holocaust?

It is clear that if I still believed in a God who has a string attached to every human being, and when one's number is up He pulls the string, then I am bound to face disillusionment. This kind of a God does not exist for me.

Obviously I am not an atheist. I have to reconcile the fact that bad things occur on this earth despite my belief that there is a God in the universe. There is a key *midrash,* (interpretation), based on a Biblical story that I interpret to illustrate my philosophy.

The biblical story is a simple one. Moses led our people out of Egypt and they were all standing at the shore of the Sea of Reeds with the Egyptians pursuing them. The people complain to Moses, saying, "Moses, why did you take us out of Egypt to bring us to this peril?

Moses cries out to God in prayer. God replies, "Moses, don't cry out to me. Speak to the children of Israel and let **them** move!"

Along comes the legend, the *aggadah,* and makes two important points:

1. There is a time for a short prayer and a time for a long prayer, and this was a time for a very short prayer. Don't bother God when **you** have to **do** something.

2. God doesn't do anything until the people themselves act.

Recently, when I was paid a tribute for some accomplishment, I replied by saying, "But that is my name, "Isaiah,"—*Yisha-yahoo.* The word *yisha* is "help," and *Yahoo* is "God."—*God will help.* My name doesn't mean "God will do for you." It just says *God will help* only after you do for yourself. Ever since I was a teenager I have believed that God would do nothing for me that I wasn't willing to participate in to the fullest.

God's Grace

When I went to seminary at Hebrew Union College, I learned that the doctrine of *God's Grace* was a minor key in Judaic thought but a major theme in Christian theology. According to the "Grace" concept, God does things for the individual because God wants to do it. Whether the individual does anything or not isn't important. God does it for God's own sake.

God's Grace is a major theme in Christianity, but a minor theme in Judaism. In my scheme of things *Grace* plays an unimportant role. I do not believe that God will do anything for me, that I, myself, am not willing to be a partner to.

An Equal Partner

Obviously, I mean an equal partner, not an unequal one. I have to do at least half the work and then God will do the other half. But why don't I do it by myself?

Long ago, I came to the conclusion that if a person thinks that he or she is the measure of all things, that God is unimportant in human life, then a person is no better than an animal. An animal is unable to conceive of a Supreme Being. An animal is unable to have a feeling of spirituality. An animal only knows the functions of life— to eat, to survive, and to reproduce.

There are other elements added to human life that transcend the generations. A dog may know its parents. A dog may know its offspring. But a dog does not know its grandparents or grandchildren.

There is something in the human beyond the animal. The person who says, "I can do it all by myself. I'm a self-made person" is, at best, an egotist.

If there isn't God in the universe, then what is the purpose of life? To accumulate all that one can in one's lifetime? To enjoy one's self and ignore everyone else is the life of the jungle.

I sense that I have something in me that is God-like, that I can either develop or push into the background. It is that element within me that has the possiblility of spiritual flourishing that I call God. God is an outside power but each individual has a God-like potential within.

There are individuals who go through their entire lives without concerning themselves with God. If you follow my theology then you understand that the difficulty in preserving the Jewish people is in preserving its religious philosophy. It is easy for the individual to adopt one of two positions:

1. Either God is the traditional God who knows and does everything, or

2. There is no God at all.

To get to the point of a modern belief in God, one must conclude that God is a spiritual being who somehow creates a spark within each person. One has to cooperate with that spark in the working out of one's destiny. One has to put selfish concerns into the background, not by being disinterested in self, but making it secondary to one's higher motives.

When we open our prayerbooks we see that the *goal of life is to live with dignity, with nobility.* That is the goal of human existence that comes from a belief in God. At the center of the preservation of the Jewish people is a belief in God that is neither the traditional one, nor the rejection of God.

How to convey this message to the educated Jewish public is a most daunting challenge.

Jewish Prayer Services

The difficulty with Jewish services is that most are too lengthy. There is a time to shorten prayer and a time to lengthen prayer. We try, at Stephen S. Wise Temple, to make our Friday night and Saturday morning services more relevant, more appealing and more interesting.

The best example of meaningful and interesting services is our own Shabbat morning *minyan.* The words of the prayers are repetitive, but the songs are not, so the service moves. It has become an exciting service and attendance induces a religious experience.

On Friday night we have shortened the service considerably and during the last year or so the congregation has learned more of the responses and the melodies so that now the experience is inspirational and meaningful.

There is nothing as salutory as participating in the Hebrew melodies of a prayer even if not a single word is understood. The lively songs announce a happy occasion, the mournful ones induce a sad moment or two, and those in-between portend a meditative mood. The melodies draw in the individual.

A Once a Month Solution

In all surveys, Catholics attend services most in the United States, Protestants second-most, and Jews are way behind.

In Los Angeles there are three congregations, two of which are off-shoots of one called the Performing Arts Synagogue. Their membership is made up mostly of people in the entertainment industry. Each congregations has services once a month and their services are very well attended. It is my hope that every member of our congregation attend services at least once a month.

There will be some regulars who attend every week, some at Shabbat morning *minyan*, some on Friday night. If we gear our services to be exciting, and each week we cater to different groups with different ideologies, people would come at least once a month and Judaism would be a living religion to all our members.

The Relevance of Jewish Law

Is Jewish Law relevant? There are many things in Jewish law that bother me and there are insights in Jewish tradition that excite me.

I am repelled by some of the rigidities of Jewish Law. I recently received a doctorate from the University of Judaism. In my remarks I said that Jewish Law always had two opinions as to what the decision should be. There was the "rigid opinion," *(machmeer)*, and there was the "lenient opinion," *(maykil)*. To be a rigid interpreter of Jewish Law you have to be learned, you have to be a scholar. But you don't have to be wise, because all you have to do is know where to look in the traditional books, beginning with the Talmud and ending in the later *responsa* literature. Whatever you find written is the proper Jewish practice. To be a *machmeer,* you have to be learned—but not necessarily wise.

My father who was Orthodox always said, to be a *maykil,* to derive a lenient decision, you have to be learned, you have to have a brilliant mind, and you have to be wise. To find a way to see to it that Judaism speaks to the needs of the contemporary generation, you really have to be learned and wise at the same time.

It is clear to me, that for Judaism to have survived this long, the lenient decision usually won out in the past. I believe this is why, in the course of 4,000 years, we evolved as we did.

I have come to the conclusion that if Reform wants only to change Jewish law as the Conservatives do, we will never succeed. Sooner or later the people will progress in their practices beyond the restrictions of Jewish Law.

When I spoke to the board of the University of Judaism, I told them of the discussions I used to have with my father. He used to say that such-and-such is according to the Law. I would immediately assent and say, however, that the custom supercedes the Law.

If we go to Jewish tradition and we find that *such-and-such* is the Law, that doesn't mean that it should be applied today. Most of the time, the way Jews practice Judaism is more relevant than the Law itself. The example that I gave is the issue of *Patrilineal Descent,* where a child who follows the religion of the father, if he/she is raised in the Jewish faith, is declared to be a Jew.

Patrilineal Descent

Recently, at a Conservative Rabbinic convention, seventy-five percent voted not to accept *Patrilineal Descent*. They knew that the Reform movement had been practicing *Patrilineal Descent* in reality for fifty years and adopted the practice in a formal resolution about fifteen years ago.

I said that fifteen years from now most Conservative Rabbis will accept *Patrilineal Descent*, because the custom supercedes the Law. The president of the Jewish Theological Seminary was sitting in the room. Rabbi Schulweis, a prominent Conservative Rabbi, came to me afterwards and said he believed it wasn't going to take fifteen years.

Who is a Jew?

I hark back to David Ben Gurion's definition of who is a Jew. Ben Gurion said that whoever honestly calls himself a Jew, is a Jew. If I look upon myself as a Jew and I've been brought up that way, I'm Jewish. And traditional Jewish Law, (where the child follows the religion of the mother), compared to the actual experience is outflanked.

Reform and Conservative

I said to the board of the University of Judaism that a generation from now there will be little difference between a Reform and a Conservative Jew. The movements may still be separate only because the national organizations have vested interests.

Even today it is hard to tell the difference between a member of Stephen S. Wise Temple (Reform) and a member of Valley Beth Shalom (Conservative).

We have about sixty of their youngsters in our high school. I asked the teachers if they can tell the difference in the youngsters who come from Valley Beth Shalom and those who come from our Temple. The teachers told me that after a week, nobody knows and nobody cares whether the children are Conservative or Reform.

When Conservative youngsters become Bar/Bat Mitzvah many of our youngsters have to sit through a three-hour service in a Conservative synagogue. That's the difference.

The High School Years

In the past I have delivered many sermons about the importance of the high school years. According to the demographers if we project the present trends to the year 2025, which is less than 30 years from now, the Jewish community in the United States will be greatly reduced. We now have five and a half million Jews in the United States. At the end of the Second World War we had five and a half million Jews in the United States. While the general population has more than doubled, the Jewish population has remained static. If all the people who were born of Jewish parents after the Second World War had remained Jewish, our population now would be between eight and nine million Jews.

If we carefully follow the studies we see that most Jewish youngsters are Bar/Bat Mitzvah, but that the ceremony doesn't mean very much. The early years are good for foundations, but the critical years in Jewish life are the high school ones. Unfortunately, it is in the high school years where we suffer Jewish attrition.

The late Shlomo Bardin, who established the Brandeis-Bardin Institute, knew this fact. He established camps for college students and he dreamed of a Jewish prep school for high schoolers. I believe that high school Jewish education is the area that will determine whether there is a viable non-Orthodox Jewish future in the United States. That is why we are putting so much of our energies into our high school.

We all know that when a Jewish youngster goes away to college, it is there that potential spouses are met. A good Jewish foundation is necessary if we want them to look for Jewish relationships. If there are youngsters who are active in a congregation in the high school years—not only in an all-day high school—but also in youth groups or summer camp, then they will be armed with excellent preservatives of Jewish tradition.

Now we encourage high school seniors to attend seminars at UCLA to help them choose the colleges to which they should apply. At these seminars it is pointed out that certain colleges have small Jewish populations with minimal Jewish programs, and that the student who wishes to remain Jewish should avoid those schools.

New Jewish Families

Potential college students are advised to go to a college where there is a sizable Jewish population and a Hillel organization with Jewish activities. If there is involvement in the high school years with Jewish affairs, the chances are better that relationships in college will also be Jewish, and if a marriage results, a new Jewish family will be created.

That is the key. It is no longer whether my son or daughter marries a Jew. The question is whether the family that ensues from that marriage will be Jewish. Although it is not foolproof, the youngster who has been Jewishly involved in the high school and college years has a lasting attachment to Judaism.

A few years ago, at the same time as the intermarriage rate of Jews in the United States hit 52%, a study came out on the intermarriage rate of the graduates of a Jewish high school in New York City and it found that the intermarriage rate of the graduates was only 6%. Of the 6% who married someone of a different faith, half of their spouses converted to Judaism and lived as Jewish families.

The high school years are pivotal to the Jewish future. It is for this reason that we risked the financial structure of Stephen S. Wise Temple when we embarked on our high school program. We accumulated a budgetary deficit of $1,250,000, but now, in our fifth year, are finally in the black.

Performing Mixed Marriages

I do perform mixed marriages. But one should understand under which conditions I perform them . . . only if I am assured that the resulting family will be Jewish.

Sometimes conditions preclude the prior conversion of the non-Jewish spouse. My sole criterion is—will it result in a Jewish family. If so, I will officiate at the marriage ceremony and work with the couple on active participation in Jewish life.

Sometimes there is an extenuating circumstance in which the non-Jewish person cannot convert to Judaism at that particular time. In one instance the father of the non-Jewish partner was the minister of a local fundamentalist church. If she had converted, the father would have lost his job. So the daughter said that she would be Jewish, the household would be Jewish, she would take the Introduction to Judaism course, but she couldn't go through the conversion because that would ruin her father. Since I'm a Reform Rabbi, and have the option of officiating or not, my sensitivity to the particular situation convinced me to do the marriage ceremony. The couple is now active in our congregation. No one can convince me that I violated the spirit of Jewish Law.

To do an intermarriage takes at least five hours of counseling. To show the couple that I really don't want to reject them, I say to mixed couples, "If you are not ready to take the eighteen week *Introduction to Judaism* course and not ready at the end of the course to say that your children will be raised Jewish, I'll give you the name of a Rabbi who will do your wedding without any conditions.

By saying that to potential mixed marriage couples I have found that only 10% choose an outside Rabbi rather than go through the course. But at least when the 10% go elsewhere it is their decision. Stephen S. Wise Rabbis haven't rejected them. We have said to them that these are our values, these are our standards and unfortunately we can't participate in something that we don't feel whole-heartedly a part of. The couple is welcome to become a part of our congregation. We will do everything possible to make them feel at home.

There are certain places in the United States where the mixed marriage rate has exceeded 80%. We have to take two steps immediately:

1. We should keep our Rabbis involved with inter-marriage couples.

2. We should advertise that we have *Introduction to Judaism* courses for all who are interested.

In our day school we have a sprinkling of youngsters who are not Jewish. Parents send their children because we have an excellent school. They know that the children will get a good education. Our school provides a positive cultural atmosphere and we do not indoctrinate. The children who come to the day school are surrounded by a wholesome Jewish atmosphere.

We have family services. The non-Jewish children are not forced to come, but most do attend. We have model Passover seders for every class. Obviously, the non-Jewish children participate. One year a little Chinese girl recited the *Four Questions*. In the room stood her grandparents in traditional Chinese outfits, not having the slightest idea what the child was doing, but beaming proudly.

If our Temple and our schools are a magnet attracting non-affiliated families and even a sprinkling of non-Jews to the beauties of our services and the excellence of our schools, then we will be rewarded for all our efforts to make Judaism exciting and relevant to our contemporary civilization.

A Symphony Orchestra

Most people in America think that this country is a melting pot. A melting pot is a huge cauldron into which we put various elements and when we stir it up together we get the end product. The product is a stew, all mixed together.

I have always believed that America is not a melting pot, but, rather, a symphony orchestra. In a symphony orchestra are various players. There is the string section, the percussion section, the brass section, and the woodwinds. It is only when these sections play together that we get a magnificent symphony. But the symphony is beautiful only because each section plays its own part. The blending together makes the symphony, but the playing of each of the parts adds to the artistry.

I believe that in this symphony orchestra that we call America, one section should be played by Jews. Therefore, Jews should be Jewishly literate, know Hebrew, know their history, and understand their religion to be able to properly play their part.

One of my achievements when I was below the age of sixteen was to get Hebrew into a dozen different high schools in the city of New York. Then I went to Brooklyn College, which had a 90% Jewish student body. I went to the dean and asked for Hebrew courses. He told me to sign up at least twenty advanced students, which I did.

I believed then, and I still believe today that America is a symphony and that we Jews have our part to play and our contribution is enriched through the instrumentality of Hebrew. Unfortunately most Jews don't know the notes. I and others, are dedicated to teaching Jews Hebrew and Jewish culture as our contribution to American civilization so that every Jew can proudly play his or her part.

I have been a Rabbi for fifty years. It has been a magnificent journey that has afforded me boundless areas of creativity.

I believe I have served my people as a whole, and individuals in times of need as well as on occasions of rejoicing. Life, to me, has been a challenge.

There are yet additional mountains to climb.

✡

Chapter Nine

Israel and Peace
A Final Word

I CAME TO THE RABBINATE because of my pressing desire to help my persecuted people. Afro-American clergymen have been the leaders of the struggle for Black equality here in the United States. It is not surprising that two American Jews who were foremost in the struggle for the establishment of the Jewish State in 1948 were Reform Rabbis—Stephen S. Wise and Abba Hillel Silver.

In my small way, I have followed in their footsteps and have always been identified as the most Zionist-Reform Rabbi in the West. My policy has always been to support the government of Israel whether led by *Labor* or *Likud.* I adhere to that policy, even today.

But these words are being written on the day after the Anti-Terrorism Summit called by President Clinton of America and President Mubarak of Egypt. While I wholeheartedly support their aims, I have several cautions with regard to the *Peace-Process.*

Let me clearly state that I have supported the *Peace-Process* until now. I still think that *Likud,* by not wanting to deal with Arafat, has no one with whom to work toward peace. But Arafat's unwillingness or inability to control terror leads me to the conclusion that the road in the ensuing *Peace-Process* ought to be travelled slowly and cautiously.

I believe that Israeli security must come even before more steps are taken along the road to peace. If Hamas and other small terrorist groups find haven in the Arab autonomous territory, then it makes little sense to proceed on any second Israeli withdrawal. But should Arafat and the Palestinian authorities imprison the members of terrorist groups without releasing them in a short period of time, (which they do now), then even Jerusalem is eventually negotiable—but not to become a divided city.

Let me not be misunderstood. I believe Jerusalem is and should remain the capital of the Jewish State. But if peace prevails over a given period of time, then it might provide offices for the Palestinian Authority—but under Jewish control.

However, unless and until Arafat confronts and eliminates Hamas, I would be against any further territorial compromises.

Nor do I think Israel ought to pursue the Syrian track any further. It is clear that one negotiating point after another has already been yielded to the Syrians, yet Assad did not see fit to attend the Peace Summit, or to reject terrorism. Nor has he moved to oust terrorist organizations from Syria or Lebanon. I believe that Assad negotiates with America but hopes for a revival of the Communists in Russia so he can pursue his belligerency with Israel. To give him the Golan, which is a natural defense for Israel, I believe would be foolhardy.

To risk Israeli security for an illusory comprehensive peace is dangerous. Israel already has growing relationships with many Arab countries. Even America can't change the hostile foreign policies of Iran, Iraq, Libya and Sudan. A treaty with Syria would not make a comprehensive peace, and the risks far outweigh the benefits.

I have other areas that concern me gravely with regard to sacrificing values in the pursuit of peace.

I do not believe that the settlements should be removed. Why should Arabs be allowed to live in a Jewish State, but Israelis not be allowed to live in Arab controlled areas?

Will the *Labor* Prime Minister of Israel yield control of non-Orthodox conversions to the Orthodox political establishment, if they will, in turn, support his peace overtures? Or conversely, will *Likud* yield to the Orthodox if they will join in forming a government under *Likud* control?

Either of these last scenarios would disenfranchise Conservative and Reform Jews in Israel, and offend Conservative and Reform Rabbis in America whose conversions would not be recognized.

To me, a united Jewish people, albeit honoring pluralistic Jewish beliefs, should not be sacrificed on the peace altar.

My overall view on Israel is simply that Jewish peace is more important than a so-called comprehensive peace between Israel and Syria. And Jewish unity and inclusion is more important than *Labor* or *Likud* forming a government by yielding on the issues of modernity to the Orthodox establishment that would restore Medievalism to Judaism.

I would like to see the day when all Jews, whatever their religious affiliation, or non-affiliation, will live in harmony and develop our unique culture and civilization.

I have dedicated my life to that end in the United States. I will fight for that result in Israel as well.

✡

Other Jewish books available from the
Isaac Nathan Publishing Co., Inc.

Books by Florence Zeldin

The American Jewish Experience, Stories of Our Roots and Branches.
Oral histories for 9-11-year-old reading. Includes puzzles, exercises and
projects. **$9.95.**

The Shabbat Shalom Book. For nursery school and kindergarden
children. A delightful Shabbat book that includes candle, *Kiddish* and
challah blessings as well as a simple challah recipe. **$4.00.**

Adult Books

A Sacred Trust, Stories of Our Jewish Heritage and History, by Rabbi
Eugene and Annette Labovitz. 2,000 years of Jewish history told through
the tales of our famous people and events. Complete with easy-to-follow
maps and time line.

Vol. I, The Talmudic Period, The Middle Ages, The Sephardic Age, $18.

Vol. II, The Silver Age of Polish Jewry, $12.

Vol. III, The American/Jewish Experience, Returning to Our Land,
   (Eretz Yisrael), **$12.**

SPECIAL — Three-volume-set, $36 — save $6

**The Art of Engagement, How to Build a Strong Foundation of Commu-
nication for Marriage,** by David W. and Sheila G. Epstein. Recommended
for all engaged and recently married couples. 3rd. printing. **$12.95.**

Threads of the Covenant, Growing Up Jewish in Small Town America,
by Harley L. Sachs. Short stories about David Katz, from his Bar Mitzvah
to his marriage, as the only Jewish youngster in a small town on
Michigan's Upper Peninsula and ten Jewish families as they struggle to
maintain their Jewish identity. **$18.**

Withered Roots, The Remnants of Eastern European Jewry, by Stuart F.
Tower. Stories in poetic form. Sections on Poland, Czech Republic/
Slovakia, Hungary, the former Yugoslavia, Bulgaria, Romania, the former
Soviet Union. Highly recommended by Steven Spielberg. **$18.**

California, Earthquakes and Jews, edited by William M. Kramer. How the
Jewish community has reacted to disasters over the past 100 years.
Illustrated with extensive index. **$24.95.**

Send checks to: The Isaac Nathan Publishing Co., Inc., 22711 Cass Ave.
Woodland Hills, CA 91364 (Calif. residents add 8-1/4% Sales Tax.)

We pay all freight and handling costs!

For Visa/MasterCard orders, call 1-800-6-JEWISH (1-800-653-9474)